The Urban Halo

The Urban Halo

a story of hope for orphans of the poor

Craig Greenfield

Authentic

LONDON ● ATLANTA ● HYDERABAD

First published 2007 by Authentic Media
9 Holdom Avenue, Bletchley, Milton Keynes, Bucks, MK1 1QR, UK
285 Lynnwood Avenue, Tyrone, GA 30290, USA
OM Authentic Media, Medchal Road, Jeedimetla Village,
Secunderabad 500 055, A.P., India
www.authenticmedia.co.uk
Authentic Media is a division of Send the Light Ltd., a company limited by
guarantee (registered charity no. 270162)

British Library Cataloguing in Publication Data
A catalogue record for this book is available from the
British Library

ISBN-13: 978-1-85078-727-3
ISBN-10: 1-85078-727-1

Cover Design by David Smart
Print Management by Adare Carwin
Printed and bound by J F Print ltd, Sparkford, Somerset.

For Nay: Thank you for being my inspiration, my wisdom, and my partner in crime every step of the way

Contents

Something Made Me Stop

I squinted at the boy in ragged red shorts. A glue-sniffer, I guessed, looking for the telltale plastic bag wrapped around his grimy fingers. Another abandoned child of the streets, wasted and sleeping it off in the middle of the dusty road, oblivious to the cars edging around him.

But something made me stop.

A stone's throw to my right, dwarfing the boy, sprawled an imperial five-star hotel complex, with neatly groomed lawns and sparkling swimming pools for the guests to enjoy. It was the kind of place that belonged to my former life as a corporate executive: a job that took me to the best hotels and restaurants the world over. At one time I would have been seated in the ballroom of such a hotel, presiding over an extravagant feast with free-flowing booze. No expense spared for our VIP clients.

It was a life I had walked away from.

Hidden behind the hotel I knew there was a dirty but lively slum, crowded with humanity, rats and disease. It was the last in a string of slums dotting the banks of the Mekong River, a broad brown sewer. And it was in these slums, among the urban poor, that I had rented a tiny shack and made a new life. From Brand Manager to Slum Dweller in one huge step down the ladder.

I kicked down the foot-stand of my beat-up old scooter and walked over to the boy. 'No more than eleven years old . . .' I thought to myself, and I noted that there was no glue bag in his hands. I bent down to examine him more closely and my gentle nudge caused a stirring.

His brown eyes, caked with sleep, flickered open and stared up at me. He lay there quietly saying nothing, the two of us stock-still in the midst of the traffic swirl. The only noise came from the tyres of cars on the dirt road, still slowing to pass us, navigating the potholes.

'Let's get you off this road, shall we?'

I wasn't expecting an answer, but the boy grunted. A sound that wasn't quite right.

'Can you speak?' I whispered in his ear. His lips drew back above his gums and he gave me a big toothy grin, his head lolling a bit as I lifted him with one arm under his neck. Then it clicked into place. Not a glue-sniffer, I realized. He can't speak. A mute. And by his eyes I could see he was without all his mental faculties.

A crowd of onlookers had gathered, fascinated by the tall white foreigner with curly hair crouching over some kid in the middle of the road. An old man with a cigarette balanced on his bottom lip informed me with a smirk that the boy was just a crazy street kid, mentally deficient and not worth the trouble I was going to. 'He's been hanging around these alleys for years,' he wheezed.

'Well, where does he come from? Who knows him? Where does he live?' I shot back over my shoulder, a little frustrated at their amusement.

My barrage of questions was met with shrugs and smiles. 'He just lives on the streets,' said a small boy with a bag of marbles, 'people give him food sometimes.' The kid stepped forward, dropped a marble into the grubby outstretched hand of the boy with the ragged red shorts and added, 'He's an orphan.'

This act of kindness did little to stop my heart sinking as I realized I was now personally responsible for another human being. An orphan child. With the boy perched precariously between me and the handlebars of my scooter, we drove off, leaving the bemused crowd in a cloud of dust.

Later that night I let out my frustrations. I had spent the afternoon on the phone to every Christian orphanage in town, desperate to find a place for the mute boy with the ragged red shorts. None would take a child with special needs.

'I know that mission place is only a third full . . . why wouldn't they take him?' I ranted bitterly to my wife, Nay. 'In the end I had to put him in a overnight shelter for street kids, but it's just a temporary solution really . . .'

Nay nodded and pointed out that the boy really needed a home and a family, not an institution. 'You can always bring him here if need be.' Her friendly Asian hospitality and wisdom never failed to encourage me and draw people around her. An infectious smile hid the scars of a tough past: a father killed in a senseless war, malnutrition, and finally escape as a refugee to New Zealand. Together, we had quit our jobs and come back to the war-torn land of her birth with a real sense of God's calling into this place of darkness and squalor.

The next day they phoned. In my heart I was half expecting it. The shelter lady was tripping over her words, saying that at first light my boy with the ragged red shorts had taken off all his clothes and run away. I hung up and spent the rest of the day driving the streets of Phnom Penh looking for a naked mute boy. In my guilt and frustration at losing this vulnerable orphan, I tried to remind myself what I was doing there and why. It isn't just about mercy and compassion for the poor, I told myself half-heartedly. It is also about faithfulness and obedience to God, no matter what the results.

When I found the boy still naked nearly two weeks later, cowering in front of a friend's house, it was a huge relief. This time I arranged for him to go and live with a kind-hearted Cambodian foster family. He couldn't toilet himself or even dress or wash himself, needing twenty-four hour a day, seven days a week care and supervision.

But despite the odds, he made steady progress, and in just a matter of weeks he was enunciating about four or five words, putting on weight and starting to settle down. We named him Vundy and he soon learnt to recognize the sound of my scooter. Each time I pulled up outside his new home, he came rushing out onto the street shouting excitedly one of the few words he had learnt: 'Papa! Papa!'

When Jesus moved from the most exclusive gated community in the universe to the worst ghetto in the world, seeking out prostitutes, lepers and children, he sparked a revolution in at least one man's life. My own. He inspired my journey from the corporate halls of power to the back alleys of Phnom Penh's slums and riverside squatter settlements. A journey woven around a love story with a feisty refugee girl from Cambodia who agreed to join me in a crazy adventure. A journey that would ultimately result in a ministry assisting over a thousand orphaned children just like Vundy.

Orphans in My Family

I learnt early to share my toys. My parents provided me with a steady stream of rowdy playmates: foster kids taken in for reasons of abuse, disability or family break-down. And even though sometimes I whined that they were messing up my beloved books or grossing me out with a snotty nose, mostly it was good fun.

And so it wasn't a big surprise or hassle when one day my mum told us to make space for a couple more: two Cambodian orphans, refugees from the murderous Khmer Rouge regime.

Mum told me 'unaccompanied minors' were not being allowed into New Zealand at that time, but these two orphans had attached themselves to another refugee family to fool the immigration authorities and escape the refugee camp.

Hardly off the plane, relations began to turn sour with the family they had hooked up with. So they admitted the truth to a social worker who agreed to place them somewhere else. And so it was that two traumatized Cambodian orphans slipped into the country, into my home and into my life.

John and Anna, with newly adopted names to match their newly adopted country, arrived on our doorstep brooding and speechless, adolescent exiles from the failed communist experiment that had killed their parents and most of their brothers and sisters.

On his chest, John bore the scars of his Khmer Rouge tortures, and despite having almost no knowledge of English language he could dramatically bring to life the story behind each mark. I was too young to really understand the horror of what they had seen and been through, but I was exhilarated by the stories of survival that began to emerge as they learned a few words of my tongue.

The first story I pieced together seemed to involve sneaking out of the village each night past Khmer Rouge soldiers and swimming down a river to bring back stolen food. The river was behind a hospital and carried away all the hospital sewage and contaminated waste. Adding to the toxic hazards, the soldiers would take potshots at the river whenever they became suspicious that someone might be below the surface. But food was scarce and John had others to provide for. The nightly gamble with death was thus unavoidable.

Another tragicomic tale, communicated entirely by flapping arms, clucking sounds and raucous laughter, seemed to involve chicken smuggling and trying to keep the excitable bird quiet as he sneaked it past the omnipresent soldiers. John had retained a great sense of humour. Dark, but funny.

Years later, fluent in Khmer language and familiar with the culture, I often wish I could go back to those boyhood days and exchange tales with them in their own language, chuckle and weep with them as a friend, hear their stories properly and share their pain as I have done with many others since.

I also wish I could go back and explain some of the strange New Zealand culture to them in ways they could understand. They must have been experiencing serious culture shock. For example, I was mystified that they refused to sleep on the comfortable beds we provided, preferring the hard floor beside the bed. Even stranger to me was their method of showering, preferring to stand outside the shower and scoop water over themselves, causing minor flooding in our bathroom and major consternation for my mum.

John would squat on our lawn seemingly lost in thought for long periods of time, then without warning he would be scrambling up one of our fruit trees, reaching the grapefruit on the highest branches without any effort at all. One day, in a foolish moment of bravado, John leapt from our second storey window to a tall tree swaying several metres from our house. The branch he grabbed couldn't hold him and he plummeted down, crashing through branch after branch to the concrete below. Courageously, and a little miraculously, he got up and hobbled away with a forced smile. But because he was so stoical, it wasn't till a couple of days later that we discovered he had broken his leg. He spent his first New Zealand Christmas oblivious, in hospital.

John and Anna were from a rural, rice-farming background and their rough physicality was quite a challenge to me, an introverted bookworm of a kid. I remember the day John lured me reluctantly to a huge buzzing beehive he had discovered in the forest near our house, a place I rarely bothered entering. With a big grin, he knelt below the hive and dipped the end of a dead branch in a jar of petrol, then quickly lit it with the strike of a match. Leaping up, he thrust the flaming branch as hard as he could into the middle of the hive, seriously enraging the bees inside. A swarm of angry bees swept out of the hive straight towards me and I let loose a high-pitched scream, hightailing it out of there, with John cackling away close behind.

John and Anna fought tooth and nail, every other day. John, being older and a guy, usually had the upper hand,

and the rest of us kids knew to get out of the room fast when one of their fights broke out.

Once I remember John snatched up a screwdriver and threw it at Anna in a fit of rage. The screwdriver struck the wall inches from my shoulder and stuck fast, deeply embedded.

'Hey! Watch it!' I squawked as I beat a hasty retreat into the kitchen, shuddering with the thought that it was just inches from being buried in my back.

Anna could put up a mean fight as well though, and I remember one wrestling match where she was attempting, reasonably successfully, to tear out clumps of John's hair. At times the beatings were truly brutal and intervention was needed. One evening I watched wide-eyed as a vicious scrap between the two of them was broken up by a friend of the family, who proceeded to grapple John into a headlock and warn him in a low menacing voice to leave his sister alone. In hindsight, none of this brutality was surprising considering what they had witnessed and suffered in Cambodia, horrors which I would only later begin to grasp, and which would in time become an even more integral part of my own story.

Every year in Auckland, the Cambodian community held parties to celebrate the lunar new year around mid-April. It was the kind of thing I hated to attend. One such day in April, lifting one side of my Walkman headphones to expose my ear, I whined, 'Come on, Dad. It's so boring! Why do I have to go anyway?' I complained bitterly that I wouldn't know anyone and the food would be weird.

'Get dressed, Craig. We're all going together as a family,' my dad chided, leaving me in no doubt that we all had to go along in support of John and Anna.

Most of the evening I moped around by the trestle tables laden with Cambodian food. Big black speakers boomed distorted traditional music around the echoing wooden school hall. Anna joined a group of Cambodian adults and children dancing slowly with twirling wrists, circling gracefully in the centre of the room. Everyone was in step and it looked like fun, if only I knew the moves. The dancers drew my attention for a while.

I didn't realize it at the time but there was someone else shyly watching the dancers that day: a cute girl about my age but shorter, with her jet-black fringe cut straight across the middle of her forehead, making her beautiful eyes look even more Siamese cat-like. If I had asked her, she might have told me in slightly accented English that she had arrived in New Zealand from Cambodia via refugee camps in Thailand and the Philippines. She might have told me what it was like to be a foreigner in a strange place. If I had asked her, she might have told me what it felt like to lose a father and never know what had happened to him. But I didn't ask her, not that day. Not for another ten years.

Called to the Urban Poor

Something about my years growing up with John and Anna must have sparked the idea to take six months break from university and go to Phnom Penh. The travel bug pumped through my veins in those days. A year living in Spain when I was seventeen with an ex-cocaine-addicted Basque separatist had first ignited a passion for adventure. And now my dramatic conversion to Christianity, at age twenty, had added another, deeper layer to my desire to get out into the world. But my experience of Jesus up to that point was mostly from a point of privilege. I had really only ever needed Jesus to meet my spiritual needs. And so it was that I met a new Jesus in Cambodia.

I lived those six months in a middle class part of Phnom Penh. But my imagination was fired by the slums and squatter shacks I discovered all over the city. I spent hours visiting friends who lived in tiny thatch huts, squatting in the grounds of the local Buddhist pagoda while they pursued their tertiary education.

Somon was a student at the University of Phnom Penh where I was teaching English. He had travelled in from the countryside, where his family grew chilli and marijuana, to stake everything they could scratch together on getting an education. He had big watery eyes that looked sad and kind at the same time and he always wore the same threadbare shirt and faded brown trousers.

Somon was dirt poor and homeless, barely meeting the fee payments for his course with nothing much left over for food and accommodation. He scraped by with the help of Buddhist monks who allowed him to stay in a tiny mud-floored, thatch shack in the grounds of the local pagoda and shared their food with him.

We became good friends and one weekend he invited me to travel with him to meet his family in the countryside. On the road we spent hours talking about all kinds of things and then the conversation turned to what was on my heart, the good news of Jesus Christ. Somon listened carefully to what I was sharing, then he turned to look me in the eye with a sad smile and asked me a question I have since been asked many times by Cambodians, 'Craig, I am very poor. What can Jesus do for me?'

At the time, I felt that Somon was slightly missing the point, asking the wrong question. I didn't see that his poverty had a lot to do with God's offer of eternal life. My modern dualistic worldview separated body from spirit, science from faith, and the natural from the supernatural. And so I explained to Somon that God was offering him a chance to go to heaven when he died – and that this offer is available for rich and poor alike. Somon's furrowed brow suggested dissatisfaction with my answer. He shook his head sadly and insisted, 'I am very poor. I am very poor.'

Later that night I tossed and turned in bed as I mulled over his question. I knew that the gospel was indeed about eternal life. But was my God only interested in saving us after death? What kind of faith was I offering Somon? He was clearly not interested in an abstract theology, disembodied and disengaged from his physical world.

It was encounters like this that forced me to think more deeply about the nature of the kingdom of God and what Jesus was really on about. I began to meditate on the words and life of a new Jesus, the Jesus who had nowhere to lay his head and walked the dusty roads with his disciples declaring that he had come to bring healing and 'good news to the poor' and promised 'blessed are you who are poor'. What would this Jesus say to Somon?

I carefully observed how various missionaries attempted to reconcile the extreme poverty of Cambodia within their ministry. Many, like me with Somon, essentially ignored it, believing that their job was simply to preach the gospel of salvation from eternal damnation and leave the feeding of the hungry to the secular agencies. They separated proclamation from demonstration. Others tried various ways to combine preaching with ministry to people's physical needs. Some of these missionaries fed the hungry in order to ensure an audience for their gospel presentation, thus creating 'rice Christians'. Others felt they should carry out social work for its own sake, without using any words about Jesus, lest they be accused of proselytizing.

None of these positions seemed very satisfactory to me. I was looking for a more integrated spirituality where proclamation and demonstration went hand in hand. The new Jesus I was discovering in the gospels walked and lived amongst the people he was ministering to, healed the sick, fed the hungry and preached justice and holiness.

My frustration was compounded when I invited Somon to my home. The place was basic by Western standards, but he was overawed, asking the price of everything in the room. I was becoming convinced that the very essence of mission is communication and at that moment it struck me forcefully that my lifestyle was communicating far more to him than my halting words in Cambodian language. Somon's utter indifference to what I said and rapt preoccupation with what I had, caused me to seriously rethink my worldview, my approach to missions and my understanding of the gospel. The criticism of Mahatma Gandhi seemed apt, 'I have told my missionary friends, noble as you are, you have isolated yourself from the people you want to serve.'[1]

By the end of that six months I still didn't have many answers. But I was convinced that God wanted me to return and live in a more simple fashion among these people for a time, to learn more about what it means to be poor in Cambodia, to learn what bringing good news to the poor might mean in the slums of Asia. I believed that God was calling me to move right in alongside them, to share their struggles and their joys. And I wanted him to show me what he was doing and saying in that place of struggle and squalor.

And so I returned to New Zealand with a new sense of vision and purpose, fuelled by youthful idealism, the spark of God's heart for the poor and a healthy dose of naïveté. Just months from finishing my university degree I believed it wouldn't be long before I could get back to Cambodia and begin my mission career. I just didn't bargain on Nay sweeping me off my feet.

It was a set-up, we know now. I had been invited to speak about my time in Cambodia at a little Baptist church one balmy weeknight and Nay had been invited to share too. My first impression, if you don't count the time when we were both young teenagers, was of a gorgeous, petite but feisty Chinese-looking girl walking up to the front of the church, struggling on tiptoes to see over the pulpit. My mouth must have dropped open as she shyly began to share her remarkable history of escape, life as a refugee and then nurture within the church community that had sponsored her family to New Zealand. Then with more confidence, Nay shared her sense of calling to return to Cambodia, a calling she had cherished since childhood. As Nay spoke of her deep longing to return to the broken and torn land of her birth and serve her own people, I somehow knew that this cute girl would one day be my wife.

Luckily, I managed to hold myself back from rushing up to her afterwards to disgorge my revelation. Instead, I determined to play it cool, casually dropping the fact that the blonde female I had arrived with was 'just a friend'. Then I offhandedly invited her to a Cambodian Bible study I was teaching at and she agreed to come along.

Afterwards, I enthused to my sister that I had met my future wife: 'I'm telling you, she's the one! You watch and see!' My sister just laughed at me as if I were crazy.

Several weeks and several Bible study meetings later, I felt I had played it cool long enough to pluck up the courage to ask Nayhouy on a date. There was just one problem: I hadn't worked out exactly how to say her name. These days she just goes by the shortened version, Nay, which is pronounced how it looks (she still gets mad if I say 'Nay: like the horse sound . . .'). But in those days Nay was using her full name, Nayhouy (Nay-hoo-ee). And I just hadn't quite worked it out. The point where you can still ask someone to remind you how to say their name had long since passed. But determined to ask her out anyway, I rang her house and one of her roommates picked up the phone.

'Um . . . hi. Is Na . . .' I pretended to cough and splutter, '. . . there please?'

'Do you want Nayhouy?'

'Yes!' I breathed a heavy sigh of relief.

'OK, I'll just go and get her.'

We talked on the phone and finally, a few days later, went out on our first date. After dinner, we sat on Mount Eden under the stars and talked for hours. I even had the chance to ask her again about the pronunciation of her name.

At one point Nay interrupted my witty banter with a finger to her lips, 'Ssshhh. Listen.' Floating up through the trees behind us came some beautiful harmonized voices singing some kind of worship song to God.

'Sounds like an a cappella church choir,' I whispered back, and it may just have been at that moment that we both really fell for each other.

I still don't know how God arranged for a bunch of human angels (a Pacific Island church choir we think) to go to the mountain that night for an impromptu singing session, but I have them to partially thank that within six months Nay and I were married. And then, finally, Nay began to entrust her story to me.

Child of the Khmer Rouge

Nay and I were born the same week in December 1973, both eagerly awaited first-born children. But the similarities ended there. Nay told me she was not yet two when the Khmer Rouge took Phnom Penh, marking the end of a protracted civil war and ushering in a four-year nightmare that would stretch to two decades without resolution. These Cambodian communists, led by the enigmatic Pol Pot, planned to establish an agrarian utopia. Their grand vision was to create a purely peasant society without money, education, religion or any of the trappings of modernity.

Within the space of a few weeks after the fall of the capital city, all the urban centres across the country had been evacuated and the entire population was forced to work the fields. Ultimately, a third of Cambodia's people would perish, two million people dead, one of the worst disasters in human history.

But the morning a crude band of Khmer Rouge soldiers marched into her provincial town and down the main street, Nay was playing happily outside, oblivious to the turmoil, and her mother was still optimistic that the end of the civil war would mean peace and the return of her husband. Nay thought her mother was old, but really at twenty-six years old she was too young to be a widow.

Watching the surly young soldiers clad in their dusty black uniforms from the safety of her father's noodle café, Nay felt her mother gently tugging her inside, to the safety of the shadows. Nay buried her face in her mother's bulging belly, and felt the child inside kick as if in premonition.

It was not until a few weeks later that the sense of dark foreboding returned to the roadside café. Playing inside while her mother worked, Nay heard the loud-speakers before she saw the procession. Three trucks rumbled slowly by, jammed with people who had stand-ing room only. Khmer Rouge soldiers trooped alongside the swaying vehicles, their leaders calling more towns-people to come forward: 'Comrades, all those who are highly educated and all who have experience in the pre-vious administration are urgently needed to help rebuild the country.'

Just as she was about to run outside to watch the com-motion, Nay's grandfather gripped her shoulder tightly, and whispered, 'Stay here little one, it is not safe out there.'

Nay rubbed her shoulder blade and watched as the trucks ambled on, turning not left to the town square or City Hall, but out of town and into the forest. Nay never saw any of those passengers again.

Nay heeded her mother's warning to say nothing of their true identity. Nay's father had been fighting against the Khmer Rouge for several years as a military policeman on the side of the government to keep the communists from taking over the capital city. It had been six months since they had last seen him. One afternoon, Nay sat and watched as her mother spent several hours removing any trace of their government connections from the simple wooden home they shared with Nay's grandfather and other relatives. Nay cried softly as her mother destroyed the photos of her father, but somehow she knew that if they were discovered it would mean big trouble.

Eventually, Nay curled up on her mother's lap as she lingered over the last photo and memories flooded back. 'Your father tried to get us out, you know . . .' her mother reminisced absentmindedly. 'But they could provide a place on the plane only for you, me and your father. No one else,' she muttered, shaking her head. 'I knew your father would never leave without the rest of the extended family.'

Soon the townspeople had all been ordered by the new regime to leave their homes in the city and build thatch shelters alongside the fields where they were to work. Little did Nay know, these flimsy huts would be her home for the next three years.

Long days turned into long months and Nay's father never returned. Though she secretly watched the road into town every chance she got, he had disappeared without a trace, one of the thousands of Khmer Rouge victims whose bodies were never identified. Her father never knew the baby son who was born to him late one Saturday night under the thatch roof of a temporary shelter. Her mother's muffled screams and agony were over mercifully quickly and were attended to by Nay's bustling aunties. Nay watched the miracle of birth with a mixture of terror and excitement and a wizened traditional birth attendant finally arrived about half an hour after the boy gasped his first breath.

With two young children to care for and no husband to help, food was scarce. One lunchtime, after days with nothing but watery rice porridge to eat, Nay and her tiny brother lay lethargic on the floor of the hut, sleepy in the midday heat. The children's eyes were dull and their skin dry and loose with malnutrition. Nay watched her mother kneel in tears and whisper a prayer on behalf of her children. Then her mother lay face down on the bamboo slats of the hut floor as if waiting to die, gazing with watery eyes through the slats at the dirty brown floodwaters that were beginning to rise below her tiny home. Nay was too weary herself to comfort her with a hug.

Suddenly, Nay's mother jumped to her feet and called in excitement to Nay's aunt, 'Yary, bring a stick! Hurry!'

'What? What is it?' laughed Nay, stumbling dizzily to her feet. Though it was strictly forbidden to catch anything for personal consumption, Nay watched her mother and aunt splashing through the water and, suppressing hysterical laughter, whacking at the fish in the shallow floodwaters below the hut. Nay watched in glee as victorious, the two women yanked fish after fish out of the water, beaming at their prize. That night they all feasted on the timely catch and the family thanked God for sparing the lives of their children.

The months continued to pass in a monotony of toil and quiet desperation. Nay felt sad that her mother was forced to return to the fields soon after the birth, and annoyed that though only four years old herself, she was made to keep watch over her little brother. Nay was too young really for such responsibility and once was told off severely when her mother arrived just in time to see Nay hauling the waterlogged infant out of a nearby creek.

Each night Nay would massage her mother's blistered feet in an attempt to relieve her mother's weariness. Her mother confided that she had never worked in a field before, 'Your grandparents are successful Chinese noodle sellers, city people. Our people have never been rice farmers. But you must promise me to keep quiet and never tell anyone. The Khmer Rouge wants everyone to be peasants, and that is what we must be.' Nay dared not ask about her father. She struggled to picture his face now, but his absence was a dull pain in her heart.

One day, Nay watched as a passing soldier slowed to watch her mother clumsily swinging a bamboo hoe. A smirk played on his lips and with the end of his weapon he prodded her roughly.

'Comrade, show me your hands.'

Nay winced as her mother reluctantly turned her palms up. Though now blistered and grimy, they were clearly the soft hands of someone who was not used to manual labour.

Narrowing his eyes, the soldier snarled, 'Comrade, if you are truly who you claim to be, you will certainly be able to plant this whole field with potatoes by the end of the day. Alone!' He motioned to an empty field nearby.

Nay's mother turned her head quickly to glance at the field then lowered her eyes and murmured assent. The soldier ambled over to join two other soldiers chuckling lazily under the meagre shade of a sugar palm tree.

Swinging her bamboo hoe in an arc above her head, Nay's mother let it fall heavily on the sun-baked dirt, chipping away a hole where later she would place a small potato plant. Hour after hour she sweated, intent on her task, only looking up infrequently to make sure Nay and her brother hadn't wandered too far off. Finally, late in the afternoon, she planted the last potato seedling in its hole. Nay could see she was aching and fatigued. But the soldiers were mollified for the time being and Nay's mother was free to go.

The next day however, the soldiers were back, motioning to an even larger field. Her mother's hands were badly blistered from the gruelling labour the day before, but Nay knew she had no choice. Once again Nay kept one eye on her baby brother and the other on her mother, watching as her mother slaved against time; Nay could see she was trying to ignore the pain in her back and her weeping hands. By the end of the day,

Nay's mother had somehow finished the field and mother and daughter crept home humiliated and exhausted: Nay with the toddler hoisted onto her hip, and her mother dragging the bloodstained hoe along the ground.

On the third day, the soldiers were no longer laughing. Churlishly, they indicated a much larger area, twice the size of the field she had planted on the first day. Nay's mother gingerly grasped the bamboo hoe, wincing with pain. Nay winced in sympathy as she realized the first swing would rip open the barely closed wounds from the day before. he could see that her mother's hands were slick with fresh blood. All day long her mother drudged, almost feverish with pain, and it was late in the evening before Nay watched her mother collapse into a dreamless sleep on the mat beside her.

In the morning, the soldiers had lost interest and, gratefully, Nay watched her mother hobble over to rejoin the work gang on another field, whispering a word of thanks to the unknown God who had apparently answered previous prayers.

By October 1979, Nay's family were increasingly desperate to escape the brutal regime and its diabolic foot-soldiers of death. Nay had watched hundreds of her neighbours and many of her own relatives succumb to starvation, beatings and overwork. Nay's mother whispered her fears to Nay one night. Though Nay was just five years old, she would soon be recruited into the children's work gang to work all day long in the fields alongside the adults. Nay wondered if she would be made to plant potatoes until her hands bled too and quietly sobbed herself to sleep that night.

It was rumoured that Vietnamese soldiers had defeated the Khmer Rouge further south and were getting closer every day, but the family had no stomach for more fighting and little hope that their ordeal would be over soon. They had heard furtive whispers of a truck driver who for an exorbitant price could get them near the Thai border. From there it would be a long trek through the jungle to a refugee camp. Whispered plans of escape began to fill their evenings.

One night a young cousin arrived exhausted from out of town. He came to Nay's house in the shadows of the thatch shelter.

'Your relatives sent me to get you and the rest of the family,' he whispered breathlessly. 'I can guide you to the refugee camp where they are. But we'll have to trek through the jungle . . . there are landmines . . .' he trailed off, staring at the floor. Nay knew he wasn't certain they could make it.

Finally, a few days later, under the blazing midday siesta sun, Nay's mother gathered her into her arms, stroking Nay's back and soothing her with whispers. Nay's aunt carried the boy, now a toddler, and two or three other members of the family carried bags containing their meagre possessions over their shoulders. Tears were a luxury by this stage, but Nay wept quietly again as she said goodbye to the others who weren't coming. She tried not to think that she would never see them again. Nay watched her mother tuck some gold jewellery that she had carefully saved into the hem of her skirt and the tiny party hurried off to the appointed meeting place.

The truck was hours late and Nay was wondering if they would have to return home to the thatch hut and the daily toil, when she heard the low rumble of a distant vehicle rising from somewhere over the horizon. Eventually, a rusted heap piled high with fertilizer wheezed to a stop beside them and the nervous passengers climbed into the cab. The price in gold was negotiated and the truck set off.

Before long, the driver turned to Nay's mother and poked a gnarled finger in her face. 'You're my wife.' His breath stank. Turning to Nay he flashed rotten yellow teeth, 'And you're my daughter. Nay began to cry despondently, wondering if this horrible man was to be her new father. 'You know . . .' he pleaded, conciliatory, '. . . when the Vietnamese soldiers stop us.'

The driver's prediction soon came true and they rolled to a stop at a checkpoint just a few miles down the road. He whipped off his dirty old baseball cap as a sign of respect and jerked a grimy thumb back at the manure, 'Got a load of fertilizer.' Wheeze. Cough.

A Vietnamese soldier bent slowly to peer through the open window into the cab and everyone held their breath in tense silence. Nay took her mother's lead and stared straight ahead at the road.

'Who this?' he barked in the singsong twang of Vietnamese-accented Khmer, indicating the other passengers with his pistol.

'My wife, my children, my sister . . .' The driver counted them off nervously. Nay noticed sweat patches growing under his arms and swallowed a terrified sob, a single tear rolling down her grubby cheek.

The soldier turned to his mates and spoke in rapid-fire Vietnamese. They sniggered. Then he bent down again and drawing his pistol, waved it lazily in the driver's face. He stared at him for what seemed like an age. Then he holstered his pistol and spat in the dust by the truck. 'Go. Now!' The driver hit the accelerator pedal and the truck sped off, leaving the soldiers in a cloud of red dust and truck fumes.

The sun was setting, and the travellers were tired from hours of bone-jolting driving before the fertilizer truck finally pulled over at the edge of the road and everyone stumbled out. 'This is as far as we go,' gruffed the driver. 'Thailand is that-a-way.' He pointed with his chin at a distant mountain range. 'Oh, and watch out for the landmines . . .'

Nay and her brother were tired and irritable, so her mother found a shady spot out of sight to rest and doled out some of the rice rations they had brought tucked into their bags. After a short break, they roused again and set off into the forest in the direction of the mountains.

All that day, and through the night they trudged, stopping infrequently to rest and then pressing on before they were refreshed, fearful to stop too long. Every now and then the dark night would light up with a landmine explosion, either up ahead or behind them where they had already travelled. Every step was a gamble with death. As they passed corpses, some recent victims, others just skeletons, bony fingers still clutching their earthly possessions – like a bag or a water canister – Nay's mother would cover Nay's eyes with her fingers. Nay tried hard to be brave and not to look.

Finally they reached a steep mountain pass and the only way through was by wading in the waist-deep river. Between the adults, they took turns carrying the two children on their shoulders above the water, trudging waterlogged through the muddy torrent for hours before reaching a place where they could crawl out. Hauling themselves up onto the bank the tiny party lay panting for breath. Suddenly from up ahead came the sound of muffled voices. Nay's mother motioned for the cousin to creep over and investigate.

✦ ✦ ✦

'Khmer freedom soldiers,' he whispered on his return, 'they are taking everyone's money and jewellery.'

Nay's mother sighed. 'Are they Khmer Rouge? Thai? Vietnamese soldiers?'

'No, they are speaking Khmer. But they don't wear the Khmer Rouge uniform.'

Nay's mother grimaced with resignation. 'We must go on. Behind us there is only certain death. Perhaps we can buy our freedom.' And with that she hoisted Nay onto her hip and set off. The others hustled to catch up.

A rustle, and then a barked order: '*Chup!*' Obediently, Nay and the others stopped in their tracks. Several guns were cocked and aimed at their ragged party. Nay grabbed onto her mother in fear as the soldiers surrounded and looked the bedraggled women up and down with salacious sneers.

'Please . . . ' her mother began tearfully. But the soldiers were already waving them through. Another miracle. Nay's mother gathered herself and motioned for the others in the party to hurry on.

They dared not speak for a few hundred metres, hurrying nervously out of rifle range. Then the trees thinned and they saw it. A massive tent city. Blue tarpaulin as far as the eye could see. And everywhere, people. Thousands of people. Chatting and cooking over open fires, sitting around and laughing and just going about their daily business in a massive refugee camp, a seething mass of humanity.

Nay was confused, but her mother released a cautious whistle.

'We're safe!'

And then in relief the two women, sisters-in law, exhausted and filthy, collapsed into each others arms, crying and laughing, dancing round and round in gleeful abandon. Nay at first just marvelled at the laughter and then she joined in, delighted to see everyone so happy. Nay's mother gathered her into her arms and pressed her face to her daughter's cheek with a fierce affection.

'Thank God . . . Thank God . . .'

Relocation

Every advice-giver in town told us not to head off to Cambodia too soon after marriage.

'Get a good job, earn some money, settle down, learn to live together first before doing anything drastic,' came the cautious voices.

So we did the next best thing and relocated instead to a poorer area of South Auckland to be near our Cambodian friends. We were keen to reach out to the young Cambodians who found themselves wedged between two cultures. They looked like Cambodians, but dressed and described themselves as 'homeboy gangstas' or rappers from an American ghetto and spoke like Maori or Pacific Island New Zealanders. Nay knew where they were coming from and before long we found ourselves starting up a youth group for these troubled kids.

I learned the language. Not Khmer, but a 'homie' slang mixed with a few Cambodian words. Nay learned to squeeze ten big kids into our tiny broken-down car (good practice for attempting to carry multiple people on a scooter in Cambodia). And we both learned how to walk alongside patiently as the kids made mistakes, got pregnant, and got kicked out of home, school and the local shopping mall. They taught me what they could about life as an Asian in New Zealand and I taught them what I could about Jesus.

But I was leading a crazy, disparate life. Evenings were mostly taken up with courses towards a degree in Theology at Bible School and weekends were spent with our Cambodian friends and youth group. During the day, I dressed up in a suit and tie and went downtown to work as a Marketing Executive at an international software company. It was during the technology boom and they were raking in the cash. With university degrees in Marketing and Management, it was actually a pretty good career move for me, if I hadn't been so focused on Cambodians. They sent me all over the world to run conferences at five star hotels, treating our clients to the finest of fine dining. I lasted three years.

One night at an expensive party for clients that I had organized at an exclusive restaurant nestled on the ski slopes at Beaver Creek, Colorado, I looked around the room with the surreal sense of being an outside observer. The CEO, a brutal but brilliant businessman, called me over boozily and slung his arm around my shoulder. 'Craigasaurus!' he roared (the name he used whenever I was in his good books) 'Craigasaurus, this place is incredible!' I nodded my agreement. It was incredible. Unbelievable. Ridiculous even. Mine was an odd life, mixing with the rich and powerful while living with the poor and marginalized.

One evening after work, I was sitting in a course on Urban Mission taught by bearded missions strategist and founder of Servants to Asia's Urban Poor, Viv Grigg. I loosened my shirt collar and tried to set aside the corporate world and work things on my mind. Viv shared in his uniquely quiet but compelling voice about the massive people movement that is urbanization and I thought about the cities I had visited as part of my job, rarely seeing beyond the trendy restaurants and five star hotels to the seedy side of town. He spoke of how over the past century, in every part of the world, people have been leaving rural areas in record numbers and seeking refuge in the city. My thoughts wandered to Somon and others I had met in the slums of Phnom Penh. Viv pointed out that for the first time in history, more than half of the world's population now lived in cities. But instead of finding refuge, many of these people were finding misery. More than a third of the people living in the world's largest cities were poor, powerless and dying in urban slums – and those numbers were increasing, he said. The one billion people living in slums worldwide represented the world's largest unreached people group.[2] I was struck by that phrase: 'the world's largest unreached people group'.

I took home one of Viv's books and read how he had moved into a squatter settlement in Manila and I was reminded again of my own sense of calling back to Asia. I read his challenge to God's people: 'In the next few years, there needs to be an ever-growing stream, a new thrust to these dirt-and-plywood jungles. We need bands of people who, on fire with the message of Christ's kingdom, will choose a lifestyle of simplicity to proclaim that kingdom to the poorest of the poor.'[3]

I knew then that the calling on my life, to serve the urban poor, should be in this way, with these radical followers of Jesus. I needed more details though, and so I surfed the Internet to find out how to join (www.servantsasia.org). I read with a deepening sense of excitement about the common set of five principles which unite Servants workers

- **Incarnation**: Servants workers relocate to live with the urban poor, learning from them, building genuine relationships, participating in their lives and struggles, learning their language and their culture, and working out how Jesus' love can best be shown in their context.

- **Community**: As well as a commitment to the communities they move into, Servants workers have a passion to work together in supportive teams that model the love, care and community that Jesus spoke of. They work with people, not just for them.

- **Wholism**: Since God is working 'to redeem all things' and to restore wholeness of life to rich and poor alike, Servants work for justice, proclaim God's grace, and lift all things to Him in prayer. They want to see the good news of Jesus proclaimed in word, deed and power.

- **Servanthood**: Servants workers seek to follow him who came in humility 'not to be served but to serve', the path to true leadership. They seek to empower the poor by placing control in their hands and not overpowering them with outside resources or expertise. They are prepared to embrace sacrifice and suffering, the only way to faithfully share in the life of Jesus and the poor.

- **Simplicity**: Servants workers commit themselves to lifestyles of inner and outward simplicity, setting aside the 'right' to affluence while there are still those who live in abject poverty. They desire to be a relevant yet prophetic voice in a world preoccupied with self.

This sounded like just the sort of challenge I could see myself embracing: a radical Christ-centred way of living our lives. And I sensed that somehow this approach might help address some of the issues I had encountered in my friendship with Somon and the poverty of the slums.

Viv lost no time in hooking us up with the international mission movement he had catalyzed: Servants to

Asia's Urban Poor. And so we began a new phase of our journey down the ladder, hand in hand with the new Jesus. He was taking us to meet his friends, the urban poor.

Welcome to Victory Creek Bridge

The small plane touched down jerkily on the Phnom Penh runway and an oppressive heat hit us as soon as we climbed down the airplane steps and walked across the tarmac in the blazing sun. The airport building was a small structure, housing a line of about ten customs officers who took turns examining our passports, then passing them on to the next person. We joked with them in Cambodian language and this helped speed the approval process.

Outside, I recognized a thirty-something guy waving. He was slightly dishevelled and professorial in glasses and Jesus sandals: our new team leader Kristin Jack. He was waiting to welcome us to the Servants team.

The next few days were a whirlwind. One of our first priorities was to find a place we could call home in an urban poor slum community. It was important to us that we bonded first with Cambodians, rather than foreigners. A team mate was going back to the UK so we decided to house-sit her home in the slum while we looked for a place of our own.

At the end of a narrow dirt alley, her abode was on the second floor of a simple wooden house. It looked out over a three-metre high concrete wall, topped with barbed wire, just to make sure none of us got any ideas about climbing over into the local garment factory. Most of our neighbours were young women, in from the countryside to work in the factories, though the lady next door made her living selling her plump chickens at the local wet market.

Dumping our couple of bags on the floor and looking around our temporary home, I finally located a tap in the bathroom, but twisting it elicited nothing more than a faint gurgling sound. So I left it on. Later that day an enormous liquid burp heralded the arrival of water and I rushed into the bathroom just in time to witness the constipated gushing of what looked like gravy. Our community's water was pumped straight from the Mekong River and everyone used a magic rock called 'alum' to make the silt settle on the bottom before using it. Later some team members told me the rock was made of the same chemical as deodorant.

That first night, Nay and I lay on top of the single bed, trying not to get too close because of the sweltering heat. I was beginning to have serious doubts about what we had gotten ourselves into. On the edge of sleep, a sound arose that sounded like someone was trying to sing an impersonation of a cat being slowly tortured to death. This time I didn't turn to Nay and whisper romantically about the beautiful sounds of a church choir. I cursed loudly and went out to investigate. In Cambodia, every street, even alleyways in the slums, have at least one enterprising person who has bought some karaoke videos and plugged a microphone into the back of their TV. In that neighbourhood, we were lucky enough to have two! They charged the punters a few cents per song and then pumped up the volume so the whole neighbourhood could 'enjoy' it too. Sleepless in bed that night and every night for the six months we stayed in that community I consoled myself by thinking that at least it was contributing to better literacy amongst the poor, as they strained to read the scrolling words on the bottom of the screen. God was already beginning to chip away at me.

After a few weeks, I developed a nasty rash on my arms and legs from washing in the river water, so I began to use our valuable clean drinking water, which dripped very slowly through the filter, for bathing as well. I perfected an excellent technique that used only one litre of water per shower. Our chicken-selling neighbour, however, was not worried about the effects of the dirty water. We discovered the secret of her plump chickens when Nay spotted her brandishing a huge syringe full of river water that she was injecting into her chickens to make them look fatter.

Every morning I would go out on long walks through the slums of the city, sometimes praying, sometimes just sitting around bored with the motorbike taxi guys or striking up conversations with food vendors and street kids. Hours later I would return home drenched in sweat and Nay could see in my eyes that we were still no closer to finding an urban poor community we could call home. The soundtrack to our slum existence was provided by the competing karaoke bars in our alley.

One day I wandered into a slum community known as Victory Creek Bridge. The 'creek' had long since left its victory days behind and was now just a black trickle of filthy, contaminated sludge. The houses in the community were makeshift thatch or corrugated iron shacks and wooden homes on stilts over the creek and around the bridge. I struck up a conversation with a lady selling *borbor* (Cambodian rice porridge) and eventually I told her I was looking for a house to rent.

'The villas that the foreigners rent are all in another part of town,' *Borbor*-Lady informed me with a cheeky grin.

'I don't need a villa, I'm just looking for something small for my wife and I to live in.'

'There are no houses here with air-conditioning,' she protested.

'No, I don't need air-conditioning. Just something simple will be fine.'

Borbor-Lady shook her head in disbelief and motioned me behind a thatch hut. Pointing up a rickety ladder to a padlocked wooden door, three metres off the ground built into the side of a brick wall, she smiled wryly. 'That place is for rent – twenty-five US dollars a month.'

And so we moved into our first slum home in Victory Creek Bridge community. *Borbor*-Lady was our landlady. A two-room shack, barely tall enough to stand upright, with only one window and one door to let light in, was our castle. Through the middle of our bathroom, which contained little more than a squat toilet and a bucket for washing, an unused electricity pylon which began in the house below and rose up like a turret through our ceiling, towered high above our house. We were built in, enclosed on three sides and below, and a thatch hut tottered on wooden stilts directly in front of our only window.

Sometimes at night we could hear people clambering over our rusty tin roof, and the next day we'd notice newly attached, illegal wiring, strung from our pylon, stretching over the roofs to someone's shack. Ironically, our poor neighbours in Cambodia were paying more for their electricity than the middle class or rich, simply because they could not afford the government connection fee and so were forced to purchase their electricity through middlemen who charged huge mark-ups. We joined them in paying the exorbitant fees.

To get into our home we had to climb up a rickety wooden ladder, like a drawbridge to our castle, only we couldn't raise it to escape the outside hordes. The railing would occasionally come off in our hands halfway up, leaving us waving our arms wildly trying to regain balance. There were always kids all over the ladder and we quickly came to the realization that our ladder, like most things, was considered public property in the slum. People would laze around on the bottom rung, smoking or chatting, watching people go by or observing us go about our daily lives.

One of our first visitors was the local traditional healer, or *kru kmae*. As far as I could tell, he was largely ignored by the rest of the village. He was a Would-be Witch Doctor, unpopular in our community, and he had come to see whether we would pay him some money to pray a blessing on our home. We welcomed him in and gently let him know that we had already asked Jesus to bless and protect our home.

But as we sat around in a circle on the floor of our new house, sipping water, the Would-be Witch Doctor decided to perform a little ceremony anyway. Suddenly, the old man's bloodshot eyes locked with mine over the rim of the drinking vessel. Sucking noisily from the cup, he retained the water in both cheeks and turned his head to one side. Water droplets burst in a glistening shower from his mouth, spraying half the tiny room. I was too shocked to protest. Like a video in slow motion, I watched helplessly as he pursed his lips and slurped another mouthful of water. The second spray covered the rest of the room, including a few vile droplets on my arm. Then his tongue, flecked white with spittle, darted in and out between moist lips as he muttered an incantation over our newly rented slum home. The impromptu ceremony over, he sat back and declared, 'Welcome to Victory Creek Bridge.'

Some gentle questions led into a good conversation with him about life and spirituality and he left on good terms, though we were a little shaken by our first brush with the eccentric Would-be Witch Doctor.

The next day we asked our neighbours what exactly had happened. They told us the old man really was not recognized in the community as having any spiritual powers; in fact he was greatly disliked for his vicious tongue and ferocious temper. Nevertheless, we spent some extra time praying fervently through our house that day.

Exciting encounters like this were a challenge to our comfortable Western worldview, but the daily drudgery of living in the slum proved to be a much bigger challenge. During the worst days, we began to wonder whether the cost of living incarnationally with the urban poor was simply too high. I personally needed to go back and re-examine the theological and missiological reasons for what we were doing. Thankfully, our first year in Cambodia was considered by Servants to be a formation year, a time for in-depth study and mentoring. And so I was able to spend a lot of time discussing the assigned readings and in particular our incarnational approach with my team mate and friend Kristin Jack, who had already spent several years living in a riverside slum with his wife and two children. They had once come back from an extended break to find that their tiny thatch home had been washed away down the river when the riverbank eroded. He knew intimately the highs and lows, ebbs and flows of incarnational living.

Kristin had given a lot of thought to it and even done some writing on the subject and he pointed out to me that Jesus' incarnation lies at the very heart of our Christian faith and mission. Jesus left his privileged position to join us in our human condition, suffering alongside us[4] even to the point of a degrading death. We discussed whether the incarnation was just theologically descriptive or whether it was also supposed to be strategically prescriptive, our model for mission. He reminded me of the words of Jesus, 'As the Father has sent me, I am sending you.'[5] Kristin often told me that it is from Jesus' incarnation that we learn the foundational principle of communication: *the medium is the message.* When Jesus left the comfort of heaven to live and minister amongst those he was called to serve, his life of service, suffering alongside, and his sacrifice on the cross was at the heart of his message. Likewise, the cross is not merely a symbol of atonement but Jesus' prescription for the lives his followers should lead, 'If anyone would come after me, he must deny himself and take up his cross and follow me.'[6]

It was all theologically true. 'But,' I whinged to Kristin, 'the daily reality of following Jesus into the slums is tough, isn't it? I know that mission is all about relationships, but living alongside these people in this place and being a friend and neighbour really sucks sometimes. Especially for an introverted wimp like me!' He nodded in agreement and asked what we found tough and what we were doing to take care of ourselves.

I sighed heavily and explained that Nay hated the smells and I hated the noise. Our walls were so thin that we could hear the guy next door breathing heavily throughout the night, sleeping just a few inches from us. Not to mention our initial six months of hell living in karaoke kingdom. I was pretty sure that sustained immersion in these kind of difficult conditions would result in fatigue, irritability, difficulty concentrating and ultimately burnout. Evidence of this was the overwhelming feeling that I wanted to punch someone in the face whenever they did something that annoyed me. Especially irritating were the officious whistle-blowing, baton-waving policemen who populated every street corner waiting to leap out on hapless foreigners and issue spot fines that would buy their morning cigarettes.

I really identified with the table-tipping Jesus in the temple during those early months.

Kristin encouraged me to learn good ways to minimize the impact of these negative factors, such as regular exercise, times outside the slum with team members and friends and the occasional holiday. In fact, we found that we needed to take time out very often in the early days. The first few months we would sleep in the team centre, (a place the team maintained outside the slum for occasional rest and retreat as well as team meetings), as often as one night a week. This frequency gradually reduced over time to nothing as we became used to the conditions and found our own rhythm.

We also weren't afraid to make a few appropriate changes to our house in order to increase our comfort levels. In fact, Cambodia is the home handyman's dream. You can add your own water pipes, electric lights, fans and other fixtures all over the house to your heart's content, with no worries about building codes or local government regulations. I admit to being manually challenged in this area, but nevertheless one day I decided to cut our old double bed in half to make two singles: one for guests to sleep on and one to use as a sofa. All the neighbourhood guys crowded in with excitement as soon as they saw that I was brandishing a saw. Crazy-eyed foreigners wielding sharp objects that they don't know how to use quickly draw a crowd in Cambodia.

I laboriously cut the bed in half and then it dawned on me that I was missing quite a few legs and a couple of crosspieces. After the guys had finished falling about laughing at me, we managed to rustle up some spare wood and finally I got one single bed in a presentable state. The rest of wood from the other side they were more than happy to take away to patch up holes in their own houses.

The true test of the newly-constructed bed came one day not long after, when a huge rat, doped out on rat poison, came ambling across the room with his beady bloodshot little eyes fixed right on me. In pure terror I leapt onto the single bed I had so painstakingly constructed and it immediately collapsed beneath me like a toothpick. Luckily the rat, though hazy with poison, was scared away by the almighty crash. I decided to limit my home handyman endeavours to coat hooks after that.

In the midst of this craziness, finding a life cycle that included a time of rest every day, every week and every season, became crucial to our well-being and balance, not to mention our sanity. Our Cambodian friends and neighbours would take a long lunch break, two whole hours, during which they normally had a snoozy siesta to escape the heat of the midday sun. I found it important to respect that time of rest and eventually learned to enjoy it as a time of refreshment.

Another important thing for us was to find a balance between our need for privacy and our desire to not shut ourselves off from the neighbours behind a big obnoxious fence. Cambodians have a very different concept of privacy to us and it was not easy living in the slum equivalent of a fishbowl. This added to the overwhelming feeling at times that there was no escape from the ministry. I was used to a nine to five work commitment and when it began to sink in that we were 'on duty' twenty-four/seven I struggled at times with a draining sense of entrapment. In hindsight, our very first house at Victory Creek Bridge was not quite the right place to live in that regard, a bit too exposed, a bit too fishbowl-like. And so, after about a year we shifted just a few metres away to a more sustainable house, still in the heart of the slum, but fully installed with the luxury of a door we could shut properly when we needed time out.

The rest of the team was really supportive and weekly team times, debriefing and praying for one another, were a lifeline. In time, we came to believe that with God's grace we might be able to not just survive in the slum but actually thrive.

Sometimes people asked me whether security was an issue. And initially we were quite surprised to find that many homes in the slum had bars on the windows. Other Cambodians constantly warned us that we were living in a 'bad area'. Motorbike taxis routinely refused to go all the way to our house when dropping us off. But when we moved into Victory Creek Bridge community and befriended a gang of glue-sniffers and street kids who hung out in the area, we questioned them closely about their stealing habits and they replied smugly: 'Oh no, we never steal anything from around here. We go over to the rich areas to steal!' I wanted to remind them of that implied promise when they later swiped my motorbike helmet, but otherwise in all our years living at Victory Creek Bridge, security was never a major issue for us and we never suffered a break-in.

At first, Nay and I grappled with the fact that because our lives were highly accessible to our neighbours, they had greater opportunity to make requests for assistance. We didn't want to reinforce traditional unequal power differentials or get sucked into patron-client relationships. But we quickly realized that avoiding the poor or cloistering ourselves away might temporarily circumvent the issue, but would not address the root cause of the problem.

One day, a friend came to us for help since her husband had run off and rent was due. She was asking to borrow $10. We had the money, but we knew instinctively that giving it to her would muddy the friendship. In the end, not knowing what else to do and feeling it would be incredibly stingy to do otherwise, we loaned her the money and she promised to repay us as soon as her next payday at the garment factory rolled around. The payday came and went and we could see she was avoiding us. In fact, we never did get the $10 back, but that was inconsequential to us. The true loss was of a friend who no longer felt she could be our friend because she had an unpaid debt. We told her to forget the money and just be our friend again but things were never quite the same. In her eyes there was a loss of face, a loss of dignity and a sense of indebtedness. We were learning hard lessons about poverty and charity, relationships and dignity that would one day greatly impact our wider ministry.

Through lessons like these God was also forcing me to confront the inequity between my life of privilege, opportunity and material wealth and the lives of our poor neighbours. I had been blessed with so much and I realized that for most of my life I had taken it for granted. So, for a while I swung to the other extreme. I was determined to go extra hardcore and then ended up feeling slightly superior to other missionaries because we were living such a simple lifestyle.

American friends of ours who lived in a normal missionary middle-class home once wrote a comment in our guest book that made me laugh 'You guys are missionary animals! We want to be just like you . . . except your house.'

We certainly tried to live at a similar level to our urban poor neighbours and use the same transport as the other people in our slum – a bicycle or an old motor scooter. We avoided packing in lots of furniture which would seem out of place in a small living space. We ditched the TV, which was no great loss, and used an icebox instead of a refrigerator. This simple lifestyle and repeated explanations helped our poor neighbours to understand that we had not come to amass power and influence by distributing favours. Instead they saw that we simply wanted to get alongside them as friends and introduce them to Jesus. The medium really was the message.

But though our methods were pretty good and our simple lifestyle was appropriate in a country where the poor still lack even the basics of food and shelter, my heart was not right. I was in subtle danger of becoming a Pharisee, carefully counting my lemon grass and chives while forgetting about extending love and grace towards my fellow missionary sojourners who were probably dealing with much deeper stuff than I was anyway.

One day in a team meeting, Kristin was talking about how our outer simplicity has to flow out of a deep inner simplicity. And how the aim is really to free ourselves of the clutter that stops us focusing on God. I had never thought about the simple lifestyle in quite that way before, as an internal thing as well as an external thing. It really hit me then how sinful and cluttering my smug attitude was and how much it must displease God, who had extended so much grace to me, to see me acting like a stingy child, withholding grace and understanding from others. I was deeply convicted.

And so I realized that unhealthy striving, legalism, a judgemental attitude, competing against others to be more holy or live more simply – all these attitudes needed to be brought in repentance before God on a regular basis and bathed in his grace and forgiveness. His grace was essential to help me avoid falling into the comparison trap. I learned that God's calling on each of our lives is unique (even within Servants), and we are all called and equipped to live in different contexts for his glory.

It also began to sink in that our calling to live incarnationally amongst the urban poor would have to be undertaken with a healthy dose of grace, not just towards others, but also towards ourselves. We could never live as simply as our urban poor neighbours did. We would always have a ticket home. We would always have access to outside resources if needed.

Someone once took great delight in pointing out that they had spotted us at the Western supermarket. Shock! Horror! We indulged in the odd treat (chocolate and cheese being our favourite vices) to keep us sane. And fat. I apologized for having taken a break from my hermit's existence to attend to my attack of the munchies. Our poverty was voluntary rather than involuntary like our neighbours, and we could move in and out of it at will. Thus we came to the conclusion that our lives would have to be rooted in a recognition of God's abundant love and lavish pleasure, despite our human frailty. Of course, the fact that we couldn't always live as simply as our poor neighbours, who had known nothing but poverty all their lives, didn't mean that it wasn't a worthwhile exercise to live alongside them, learning and experiencing their lives as friends and neighbours.

A couple of years after we moved into the community at Victory Creek Bridge, the Would-be-Witch Doctor lay dying of cancer two doors down from us. We had grown close to the family, especially the kids. Just weeks before, they had lost their oldest son to dengue fever, leaving just the younger son, Bo, who had Down's syndrome. Unpopular in the community, the Would-be Witch Doctor had no visitors and his wife struggled to care for him alone. His cancer of the throat and mouth had left him barely able to swallow and a huge pus-filled wound had to be cleaned daily. I watched her pour water into his parched mouth and the same water drip out a gaping cancerous hole under his chin. The stench was almost unbearable.

We visited most days, bringing soy milk which was the only thing he could stomach. And one day he agreed with a slight nod of the head that we could pray for him. From then on we prayed and shared from our heart many times about how to find peace in Jesus, with his wife listening in as we sat by his bedside. Finally the Would-be Witch Doctor passed away and we wondered sadly if he had made peace with God before he died. The monks came solemnly in orange to cleanse the house of his ghost and his widow wept. Bo ran crying to our home, and I hugged him. Not really understanding but sensing that something sad was taking place, the tears rolled down his chubby cheeks and mixed with the snot running freely from his nose. My thoughts and emotions were racing. We had lived three years beside the Would-be Witch Doctor, welcomed him and his family into our home, and been frequent visitors in his home. Had we made any difference? Was all the pain worth it?

Life in the Slum-Box

After a visit to our tiny home at Victory Creek Bridge, my father dubbed our house the 'slum-box'. It had a certain ring to it, but life was not all austerity and deprivation. We were already beginning to learn from our neighbours that our commitment to simplicity should not preclude valuing beauty and creativity. Poor Cambodians, not having wallpaper, cover their walls with magazine pages featuring photos of pretty girls. Though I had a feeling it was the guys of the house who chose that particular wall-paper style, I was impressed that even in the squalor they were seeking beauty. Of course, I suggested to Nay that we strip those magazine pages off when we moved in, considering them a bit tacky, and a fresh coat of paint helped transform the place.

Without a tree or blade of grass in sight, it was also hard to appreciate the beauty of God's creation. At Victory Creek, the ground underfoot was either mud or dust depending on the season and the only view we had was of the concrete underside of a bridge. The creek running through our community was so polluted that it had long since turned the colour of used oil and the only flowers in the slum lay wilting as offerings on altars. Sometimes I would just close my eyes and imagine myself lazing on a beautiful beach somewhere. Anywhere. Just far, far away from the concrete and the mud.

One day God answered my unspoken prayer and blessed me with a temporary 'nature treat'. I was picking my way through our Victory Creek Bridge community, avoiding the usual puddles, dog excrement and garbage. As I came around the corner, I spotted something green lying on the side of the road. Moving closer, I saw that it was a square foot of grass growing lusciously out of a thick crust of moist soil – something absolutely unseen in the slums. Pushing aside bothersome ethical questions of ownership, I hit on the bright idea to carry it home. This undertaking turned out to be easier said than done, but somehow I managed to shuffle my way home with this piece of grass and dump it at the bottom of my ladder.

And there it lay, right where I had dumped it. My very own front lawn. The neighbours thought I was crazy, of course. Especially when I gingerly took a seat on my front lawn and sat back with a smug grin to watch the world go by. Now who was the missionary with the neatly manicured front lawn!

Unfortunately, I wasn't the only one in the village who thought my front lawn was nice – the local dogs thought it was a great place to leave their fertilizer. My 'nature treat' proved to be short-lived, and it wasn't long before I was forced to give up my miniature front lawn as it had simply become too smelly.

By this time I was feeling a lot better about life at Victory Creek Bridge. We had developed a good rhythm, a healthy tension between the five Servants principles (incarnation, simplicity, wholism, community and servanthood) and the five Servants values (grace, rest, celebration, creativity and beauty) and we were beginning to see that living amongst the urban poor was worthwhile.

The first thing we noticed was that by living alongside these people day in and day out, we inevitably spent more time listening to them and hearing their concerns, especially the more vulnerable, less vocal and marginalized groups. I learned there was great value in simply listening to people as they gave voice to their suffering, whether it was their poverty, family problems, injustice from local authorities, or the effects of the Khmer Rouge years.

Rather than telling them to cheer up and look on the bright side, which would have been merely another way of belittling their experience, effectively declaring, 'Please don't tell me about your suffering, I can't bear to hear it', I was learning to really listen to what they were saying. Time, combined with observation, eventually led to a deeper understanding of the reality of our urban poor friends.

This was partly because living in the community allowed us to observe and interact with our neighbours at a variety of different times of day and year. Every now and then someone from the World Bank or the UN or some other big development agency would come down to our village to do their 'community development'. Now I'm not against the use of the latest 'participatory rural appraisal' techniques, 'logframes' and flip charts. But in their ivory tower confidence, inevitably they would always speak to the same people, missing those with no voice such as the beggars out working the streets or the street kids who slept nights in the shadows of the bridge. I hoped that these occasional visitors to our slum weren't falling into the trap of assuming that those that they met represented the Victory Creek Bridge community. Part of the problem was that they always came between eight and five, never at night, and so their interactions with the community were limited to those home during these hours.

Seasonal occurrences such as monsoon rains also made many slum communities inaccessible to all but the most intrepid outsiders during certain months. Victory Creek Bridge, like many of the major slums in Phnom Penh, became flooded several times a year, accessible only by rolling up our trouser-legs and wading.

Over the years, Nay and I learned the seasonal rhythms of Victory Creek Bridge. We realized the extent of transience in the community: who came and went; when was the community full of rural people seeking work in the off-season? When was the community quiet due to traditional celebrations that took place in the countryside? We saw change unfold over time and gained a sense of perspective that would have been impossible to acquire in any other way. We realized just how much change is under-perceived, or not perceived at all by outsiders.

Nay and I found tough times to be a great leveller and our deepest bonding with our neighbours in the community typically occurred when we all went through times of suffering together such as fires and floods, funerals and sicknesses. I wanted to say to our friends 'I have no solution to this situation, I don't know the answers, but I will walk with you, search with you, be with you.' But that would have been an empty cliché. In practice I didn't know what to say most of the time so I just cried or laughed along with them. And so, the smiles and friendly waves of people as we waded alongside them through floodwaters helped us realize that there was a bond being formed as we suffered these hardships together. When the poor became our neighbours, they ceased to be 'the target group' or 'beneficiaries' and became friends instead. At this point, our commitment to their well-being became even stronger.

But there was an emotional cost in living incarnation-ally. It is one thing to know the AIDS statistics. It is another to watch your friend and neighbour die of AIDS or some other incurable disease. A few months into our stay at Victory Creek Bridge, the lady in the shack in front of us grew very sick. One night our team mate Dr Janet Cornwall was visiting for dinner and she stopped in to see our neighbour. Janet confirmed the worst, it was cirrhosis of the liver. The poor woman looked several months pregnant. Over a period of weeks our neighbour really began to suffer, crying and calling out all day and night. Eventually the pain was too much, she actually lost her mind and her family had to tie her up to restrain her. This was a very traumatic time for her family and we, her neighbours would lie awake listening to her screaming in pain all night long, then whisper sympathetically to each other in the morning. Nay and I gave her painkillers and earnest prayer, without much faith I confess. Several times she seemed to die and everyone in her shack would start mourning and weeping only to find that she had suddenly recovered again five minutes later. When she finally did die, one corner of the funeral tent was tied to our front door, symbolically tying us into the funeral, and we participated with the community in their grief rituals. Those few weeks experiencing suffering with the community had a marked impact on the depth of our relationships and we noticed that they trusted and respected us more in the community after going through that time with them.

We also sensed that our decision to share the lives of our neighbours, such as opening our home to hordes of kids, had a positive impact on the self-esteem of the most vulnerable ones. Simply by being there and listening, we showed them that we valued their opinions, ideas and lives. We gave them the chance to communicate their pain. Our presence and our willingness to sit and listen offered them a voice. A positive word here and there communicated the value of a human being made in the image of God, especially to those who were looked down on in the community such as the disabled, children, alcoholics or the homeless.

One day I was sitting on the floor in our home cleaning up a gash on the face of a homeless boy aged about thirteen who hung around our community and was notorious for getting into trouble. A half-drunk neighbour wandered in and gave me some unsolicited advice.

'Don't bother yourself with that kid, he's just a useless glue-sniffer.'

I overcame my desire to punch him in the face and angelically responded that I thought he was certainly worth the trouble, because Jesus said whoever welcomes a little child welcomes him. That boy's face lit up at my words and he became a regular visitor to our home. He had realized that I valued him enough to waste my time on him so he must be some use after all.

By choosing to live at Victory Creek Bridge and building a friendship network there, we were sending the message that we valued the people and their community, not just as a place to 'do ministry' but as a place to live and share their lives. In this way, we were earning trust. We realized that until there is trust, nothing else of lasting value can be accomplished. Spending time with our neighbours and making ourselves vulnerable to experience some of the same hardships, we effectively 'walked a mile in their shoes.' This allowed us to gain a sense of credibility with our neighbours and they were much more receptive to our ideas, more likely to offer their own ideas (especially casually), more likely to tell us why an idea might or might not work and simply more likely to relate to us on the basis of friendship rather than as client to patron. When they started swearing at me lovingly and making jokes at my expense I knew I was making progress.

And we were earning the right to be heard. Nay had befriended a group of young women, including Sareem, a twenty-something nurse who lived with her husband in the wooden house directly opposite us. Sareem would watch us shyly, later telling us she was impressed that our home seemed to be a place that was open to anyone, important or not important in the community, though she herself would never dare enter! Nay persevered and one day Sareem did come in. She noticed a children's book about Jesus in our home. She asked what it was and Nay offered to teach her some English, using stories about Jesus if she would like. Sareem jumped at the opportunity and as Sareem and Nay got to know each other, Sareem became more and more fascinated with this Jesus we talked about who loved the poor and came to bring good news and healing to them. One day, she decided that following Jesus was something she wanted to do herself and she eventually became a dedicated disciple and co-labourer.

But undoubtedly a lot of the positive impact of living incarnationally amongst the urban poor at Victory Creek Bridge was on Nay and I. By struggling to survive alongside the poor and placing ourselves in the role of learners, we cultivated a new appreciation for the lives of the poor. We actually began to see some things from the perspective of our poor neighbours. We sensed their frustration and powerlessness in the face of injustice, such as the time when we struggled to get the local authorities to sign our registration papers without a bribe, finally giving up in failure and disgust. We glimpsed their resignation at systems that seemed designed to keep them down and relegated to the outside, and we saw their resilience through the constant onslaught of difficulties such as flooding and evictions. This was all learning that we knew God would use. We just didn't know how yet.

One morning Kristin and I sat down for our regular weekly prayer, accountability and chat time. And as we often did, ended up talking about the philosophical nature of the incarnational lifestyle. More and more, I was coming to appreciate that living incarnationally amongst the urban poor was much more than the sum of its parts. The value of an incarnational lifestyle amongst the poor was not necessarily limited to the immediate relationships developed, converts made, problems solved or insights learned, but also to be found in the symbolic nature of the act.[8] By rejecting our position of privilege and making a movement towards the poor we were encouraging others to move in the same direction and modelling a kingdom way of life that values the poor and underprivileged. Kristin and I bowed our heads to pray and I asked God for an extra blessing and anointing, that our life at Victory Creek Bridge community would influence many others. Not just in our own slum, but in other slums and perhaps even other communities all over Cambodia. I had no idea what God would do with that prayer.

Children of the Orphanages

It was a tiny boy of perhaps just four years old with huge sunken eyes, deep brown pools of sorrow, that shook me to the core. I never saw Visal wear anything but a pair of pale blue and white striped pyjamas, which became increasingly oversized on his diminishing frame.

He was the first of many children I watched succumb to AIDS. We got to know Visal and his mother through the tiny Christian fellowship we attended in the village near our home at Victory Creek Bridge slum. The worship services were punctuated by his frail, racking coughs which seemed to cause him great pain and made us all wince in sympathy. His suffering made many of the happy-clappy worship songs seem embarrassingly frivolous.

Later, Nay and I visited Visal's tiny home a few times and his jaded mother shared with us her struggles with her violent husband. Once, she complained that her husband had sold everything to get money for gambling, even the pot she used for cooking. We went home and returned with one of our two pots. Later we heard she had sold the pot herself to pay for her own gambling addiction. Eventually, Visal grew so gaunt that I could hardly look in his sad eyes. The pale blue and white striped pyjamas were like a tent on his skeletal frame. And then one day I heard that he had finally died. His short life and death had impacted me deeply.

The Khmer Rouge regime orphaned hundreds of thousands of children. My foster brother and sister, John and Anna, wife Nay and many of our Cambodian friends and neighbours were the people behind the statistics who made up Cambodia's first fatherless generation.

Living at Victory Creek Bridge, as we were drawn into the lives of friends with AIDS and their children, I realized that a second generation was being orphaned. AIDS had now become the single greatest threat facing the children of Cambodia's urban poor communities. The disease was stalking the slums and leaving another generation of children without parents. And one of the worst things about AIDS, as opposed to cancer, war or accidental death is that AIDS is more likely to take both parents, thus creating double orphans, children who have suffered through the death of both their mother and their father.[9] An estimated 77,000 Cambodian children made up this fatherless and motherless generation who had nursed their parents to their death by AIDS.[10]

The impact of the epidemic on these Cambodian children and their families was both immediate and long term. Like Visal, the majority of Cambodian kids infected with HIV/AIDS at birth by their mothers[11] didn't survive much beyond their third or fourth birthday.

But most of the children we knew that were *affected* by AIDS were not *infected* with the virus, only their parents were. The levels of care, support and protection they received steadily decreased as their parents became sicker. The parent's illness usually led to a loss of income as Mum or Dad could no longer work and the sale of household assets was inevitable as cash was redirected towards medical treatment. Oftentimes in desperation the family would seek out traditional healers, *kru kmae* like our friend the Would-be Witch Doctor, who took advantage of their vulnerability with grandiose claims and ridiculous cures such as eating live cockroaches or swallowing some magic herbs. These people didn't realize that AIDS has no cure.

All of this undermined the children's education, health, survival and development. Protection from violence, exploitation, abuse and neglect was patchy at best. Girls especially were often taken out of school to care for sick parents and younger siblings, and were also at increased risk of sexual exploitation.

Seeing families in these situations broke our hearts. But thankfully others' hearts had already been broken before us. The Servants team in Cambodia was blessed with a number of doctors, nurses and other medical people and had already begun responding to the AIDS crisis. Dr Janet Cornwall and other team members taught me not to worry too much about the distinction between merited suffering and unmerited suffering, since we couldn't presume to know whose suffering was deserved and whose was not. Attempting to differentiate just reflected the stingy belief that we could determine who should be the beneficiaries of our compassion and who should not, allowing us to dole out sympathy in a very condescending and sanctimonious way.[12] They didn't believe that someone with AIDS had to be a child or a haemophiliac in order to warrant compassion. So, instead of wasting time trying to make such divine judgements the team had simply rolled up their sleeves and begun mobilizing local Christians, in fact anyone willing to help, to minister to people living with AIDS. These people were taught to visit people with AIDS in the slums, hold their hands, pray for them, do practical chores around the house, anything to ease the burden.

One of the barefoot nurses who was helping the Servants team visit AIDS patients as a community volunteer was a cheerful woman in her thirties, Serei.

One day I asked Serei to tell me how she became involved with Servants and with a toothy grin she launched into an incredible story of transformation.

'My family are Buddhists you know, but I had heard about this Jesus and I wanted to know more.' I nodded to encourage her to go on. 'So when someone gave me a Bible I shut myself in my room one day to see if this holy book could tell me more about Jesus. I had just picked up the Bible when I heard a knock at the door, so I quickly hid the book and opened the door. But there was no one outside.' She never stopped smiling.

'Uh huh.' I was keen for her to continue.

'I sat down to read the Bible but again I was interrupted by a gentle knock at the door. By this time I was wondering what was going on because there was still no one outside! I sat down and a third time this happened, you know, a knock at the door and then no one outside. Finally I picked up the Bible and it fell open to a passage that read, "Here I am! I stand at the door and knock. If anyone hears my voice and opens the door, I will come in and eat with him, and he with me."'

By this time, Serei's story had given me goosebumps all up and down my arms and she went on to share with me how these words had made her weep and decide there and then to become a follower of Jesus, though she had virtually no idea what that meant. I was deeply moved. Soon she saw Christians, Servants staff and volunteers, visiting and praying for AIDS patients in the name of Christ and she decided this must be the true way of Jesus. Before long she was one of our best ministers amongst the poor.

Sareem, our nurse friend from the wooden house opposite also saw the way of Jesus being demonstrated amongst the sick and she began to work with the Servants AIDS homecare team in visiting AIDS patients. Because she was already medically qualified, Janet was able to train her to a higher level and she eventually became an indispensable part of the AIDS homecare program along with the other medical staff and volunteers. Nay and I, together with the AIDS homecare team, visited home after home, family after family, and in prayer with our Cambodian friends and team mates we began to ask what should be done about the children being left behind, the second fatherless and motherless generation.

Nay and I were sensing that God was calling us to personally become more deeply involved in some way. Talking and praying about it together, the first thing that came to mind was to start an orphanage. The rest of the Servants team weren't so sure and encouraged us to look at other options. But in private we excitedly began to imagine having forty or fifty cute little kids, immaculately dressed and well educated, that we could intensively disciple and invest in over several years. Children that would one day become pastors, Christian leaders, church planters or evangelists! An orphanage would be a tangible solution and easy to fund-raise for, my marketing brain told me.

Reluctantly at first, we decided to research the various models for meeting the needs of these orphaned children. Nay headed over to the Cooperation Committee for Cambodia, an umbrella organization for most Non-Government Organizations (NGOs), who had a small library of research reports. Searching the dusty shelves, she found a thin blue book with the results of an interesting study by the Khmer HIV/AIDS NGO Alliance (KHANA) which described clearly the situation of children affected by AIDS in Cambodia.[13] The children surveyed were terribly impacted by the loss of their parents to AIDS. The researchers found that after the death of a parent, these children were often denied rights to their parents' land, housing, and other assets. The study also found that children of infected parents were likely to suffer high levels of stress and stigmatization.

- About one in five children had to begin working to support their family.
- A third ended up caring for their parents and were forced to take on major household responsibilities.
- 40 per cent had to leave school and lacked necessities such as food and clothing.
- And nearly one in three had left home or been sent away from home.

When Nay showed me the report, I wondered aloud what happened to those children who were no longer able to live at home.

A young American woman, Sarah Alkenbrack, was doing research into the psychosocial situation of Cambodian orphans and vulnerable children affected by AIDS. Sarah told me she had compared children in 500 households affected by AIDS with a comparison population of 500 neighbouring households not affected by AIDS.[14]

She confirmed that Cambodian children in families affected by AIDS saw household income drop significantly. She also found that these children were having fewer meals per day than their neighbours' children.[15] Using an interesting measurement for well-being called the KINDL Index, Sarah assessed the quality of life of the kids in these families and compared them to their neighbours. Children affected by AIDS were found to have a significantly lower quality of life than their neighbours.[16]

Sarah came to the rather obvious conclusion that HIV/AIDS was placing a real burden on affected

households. She pointed out to me that children shoul-
dered the burden in a number of ways including being
taken out of school to care for sick relatives, lower food
intake, stigma, discrimination and lower quality of life.[17]
I nodded as I recognized these factors amongst our
neighbours and the families we had visited.

Around the same time I also met Ken Carswell, a
bespectacled young Englishman who was similarly
researching the psychosocial needs of orphans and vulnerable children in Cambodia. His study looked at 190
orphans and vulnerable children living in Cambodian
communities, primarily in households affected by
AIDS.[18]

Ken told me that these kids were impacted in a number
of ways by their parents' death. Almost half the orphans
had less food and money than before bereavement and
more chores. A third became responsible for the care of
siblings and about one in ten became homeless.

Fascinatingly, despite the difficulties, the orphans in
general reported feeling loved and cared for at home.
Only a slightly higher number than the comparison
group were unhappy living in their present environment.[19] Ken concluded that most Cambodian orphans
living in the community are in general psychologically
healthy, unless they were in physically or verbally abu-
sive situations, or living with a caregiver with a high
level of distress.[20]

I was disappointed that these two researchers only
looked at children orphaned and living in their original
communities. What interested me greatly was the situation of orphans living in orphanages. George Mueller
came to mind. His heroic prayer exploits in the pursuit
of his calling to care for orphans were an inspiration to
me. Surely these poor orphans would be better off in a
nice orphanage.

We discovered that although orphanages are rare in the West, the number of kids living in orphanages in poor countries is growing: an estimated 8 million children worldwide.[21] The Cambodian government and a significant number of secular and Christian organizations, missionaries and churches have established orphanages for Cambodian orphans. In fact, it soon became obvious that the traditional orphanage has been and continues to be widely seen by adults as the preferred option to care for orphans in Cambodia.[22]

But I was more interested in what the kids themselves had to say about their preference. I found one answer after looking more closely at the KHANA study mentioned before.[23] In contrast to adults, who overwhelmingly supported the idea of institutional solutions for caring for orphans, the children surveyed invariably preferred family and community-based approaches over orphanages.[24]

I remembered a conversation on one of my visits to a family with a teenage girl named Sonti. Sonti and her two younger brothers had been placed in a Christian orphanage by their mother who was dying of AIDS. One day I was visiting their mother who was very thin and just weeks from death. To my surprise I met Sonti, who was helping wash the dishes, and I asked her whether she was still living at the orphanage, which was run by a well-known Christian mission group with dozens of orphanages throughout the country. Sonti scowled and mumbled something about not liking it there. I decided to press her for a clearer answer.

'Tell me again why you escaped from the orphanage. It was a Christian orphanage, wasn't it? They were Christians, weren't they?' I quizzed. Sonti wiped a tear from just below her eye and looked at the ground. 'Yes, the pastor and his wife were nice to us, but the other

staff, the ones who took care of us every day, were
Christians by name only. They wouldn't let me go to be
with my mother and father who are sick.' I even begged
them, crying, "My mother is dying. Why won't you let
me go to be with her?" It was like being in a prison. The
rules and regulations said that we could not go outside
the orphanage gates except for school. No exceptions –
even to go to care for my dying mother. If we dared to
go out, they beat us with sticks.' She looked up at me
defiantly. 'I would rather have no food and be with my
family, than have plenty of food and nice clothes and
live in that place. At the orphanage they continually
went on about how we were one big family, but it
wasn't like a real family. There is nothing that can compare to the warmth and love of my mother.'

I spent several days with a couple of UNICEF consultants who were conducting the first comprehensive
survey of ministry amongst orphans in Cambodia.
These consultants counted twenty-one government
orphanages and eighty-eight orphanages run by chari-
ties and other organizations such as churches and mission groups. Combined, these groups had over twenty
thousand Cambodian children in their care.[25] Knowing
that the UN had estimated at least seventy-seven thousand children orphaned by AIDS alone in Cambodia,[26]
I wondered who was looking after the other tens of
thousands of children; 57,000 AIDS orphans was a significant shortfall. Not to mention children orphaned by
other causes.

After surveying these orphanages, the UNICEF guys
concluded that the number one reason for children's
entry into these institutions was actually not orphanhood

but poverty. Looking through their data I was amazed to discover that the majority of children in orphanage care in Cambodia had at least one living parent, if not two. Since the Cambodian word for orphan is *kmeng kombria*, which is used to describe anyone who has lost one or both parents regardless of age, it made sense to a certain extent. But, digging further through their survey data, I found that out of more than twenty thousand children in care, only 2,265 were known to have lost both parents.[27]

And so I slowly began to come to terms with the fact that orphanages in Cambodia were not really catering specifically for orphans, in the English sense of the word. Instead, the largest number of children living in orphanages were there because their families were too poor to take care of them.[28] It may have been Mum, it may have been Dad, it may have been Grandma or Aunty; someone decided that the child would be better off in an orphanage than at home, because times were tough.

Eventually, I was able to visit a large number of the orphanages in Phnom Penh and I saw that these findings were generally true. For example, on one visit to a very large and wealthy orphanage run by an international Christian mission and catering for hundreds of kids, I was surprised to find it mostly empty. That is, until the Cambodian staff explained to me that it was the week of the Khmer water festival and most of the kids were back at home visiting their parents and other relatives.

On another occasion, a lady at church was showing off a photo of her children. Leaning over someone's shoulder to take a look, I asked, 'Who are all the other children? And who's that white guy?'

'Oh they live in an orphanage. That white guy is the orphanage director,' she replied nonchalantly.

For research purposes, Nay and I decided to pay a visit to the orphanage concerned and it turned out to be a lovely missionary couple who had come to Cambodia from Europe with a vision to start an orphanage. We wondered out loud why they had taken in our friend's children.

'She is too poor to look after them.' They shrugged. 'We didn't know what else to do to help.'

Other data from the UNICEF guys revealed that there was an over-representation of boys in these institutions,[29] probably because in Cambodian society girls are considered more useful in performing housework and therefore more likely to be accepted and cared for by extended family or parents. Also, because living in an orphanage is perceived as a privilege by Cambodians, it was generally thought that families sometimes chose to send school-aged boys into the orphanage in order to take advantage of the opportunities for education, medical services and accommodation. In support of this hypothesis, the UNICEF guys observed that once a new orphanage opens in an area they would invariably experience great demand from poor local families who viewed the institution as a good opportunity for their children to receive basic accommodation, medical care and education.[30] The stories fabricated to gain entry would have made your eyes water, they said.

I found that the traditional orphanage is not the only model of orphan care in Cambodia. One of the most popular approaches advocated by secular organizations is pagoda-based care. A number of organizations were working closely with Buddhist monks to assist them in providing care to orphans and vulnerable children. There are over three thousand Buddhist pagodas throughout Cambodia, and monks have traditionally taken in orphaned boys in Cambodian society[31] but, setting aside the obvious religious issues, I had serious concerns about this approach for a number of practical reasons.

An obvious difficulty was that girls were usually not accepted, which resulted in siblings being split up and family ties being weakened. Of 167 Cambodian orphan children living in pagodas surveyed in one study, only nine were girls.[32] Reading the results of the study I felt sad for the nine girls mentioned. For such vulnerable little things, living in a male-dominated context surely wasn't healthy or easy.

Concurring with the researchers, I doubted very much whether the psychological and emotional needs, let alone the spiritual needs of the orphans living in these pagodas could be adequately met. After all, monks do not make a personal decision to become caregivers to orphans. Simply by entering the monkhood, they become caregivers by default, whether appropriate or not, whether they want to or not. There was no way to conduct background checks on the monks providing care, even if these were required by the temples. Therefore, it was highly likely that there were many monks who were not suitable for caring for children, or who simply didn't want the responsibility.[33]

The situation of the kids in these temples could be seen played out in pagodas all over Cambodia. They were more or less just present, living separate lives from the monks most of the time (except when they were expected to serve the monks). The children did not get much positive attention and were not well regarded by the majority of the temple population. It was little wonder then that their behaviour was publicly perceived as unruly, and that they were branded 'temple dogs' by the general populace.

Our research on the situation facing orphans in Cambodia was uncovering some interesting insights. As

I trawled through other research data and saw firsthand the lives of orphans living in the temples and in the community, I began to wonder if our initial optimism about the orphanage idea was misplaced. I decided to look further afield at what researchers in other countries had observed about caring for orphans.

What I discovered was that vast amounts of research had already been carried out in the fields of psychology, sociology, medicine, education and community development into the impact of orphanage life on children. Literally dozens, maybe even hundreds of these studies had been conducted over the past few decades, virtually unanimous in their critique of orphanages. Some of the most interesting and useful studies compared children in orphanages with similar orphans living in the community.

I eventually ended up compiling a summary of all the studies. Some stood out as indicative of the variety of emotional, behavioural and psychological problems that can arise.[34]

For example, researchers from the Yale University Child Study Centre conducted a five-year study comparing 75 infants in an orphanage with 75 infants brought up in foster families. The orphanage was a three-storey building, clean and in good condition. The children were provided with nutritious meals and excellent medical care. The researchers, Provence and Lipton, noticed that the institutionalized children did not play with toys as spontaneously as the foster children and were comparatively slower to develop speech. Other areas of development were also delayed in the orphanage children, especially social maturity. After being placed with foster families, these same children made dramatic gains, though there were some residual effects on their ability to form appropriate emotional relationships, particularly with men.[35] The kids were touch-starved. I saw this idea of 'touch-starvation' emerging again and again as a theme in many of the studies.

Reading these depressing indictments on orphanages I began to think of reasons why these researchers might have come up with such gloomy results. Perhaps, I thought optimistically, the negative impact of institutionalization on orphans was limited to children in large institutions. A cosy little family-style orphan home would be all right surely, and solve the problem of the children being touch-starved. I knew that increasingly people had been avoiding the term 'orphanage' and opting for more cuddly family-style names like 'children's home'.

But no, another study looked at 776 children in English 'group homes', set up to mimic a family atmosphere with between eight and twenty children in each home and an assigned 'mother'. The researchers, Yule and Reynes, still found that emotional and behavioural disorders were significantly more common in these children than in the general population.[36]

I then turned to the medical field to see if there was much research into the medical impacts of living in an orphanage. I found literally dozens more contemporary studies documenting medical and psychological abnormalities arising from institutionalization. These included physical and brain growth deficiencies, cognitive problems, speech and language delays, sensory integration difficulties, social and behavioural abnormalities, difficulties with inattention/hyperactivity, disturbances of attachment, and a syndrome that mimics autism.[37] Fascinatingly, one of the distinguishing features of the quasi-autistic syndrome reported in these orphanage children was that the symptoms improved dramatically following adoption.

Searching for the reasons behind these disheartening results, a classic book by David Tolfree came into my hands. After surveying orphanages in twenty countries over a period of three years, he summarized five reasons for these negative effects of orphanage care on children.

- Children in orphanages lack opportunities for close relationships with trusted adults, particularly men, and this impairs children's capacity to make and sustain relationships with other people. Basically, kids need a dad or a father figure of some type, as well as a wide range of adult relationships.
- Children in orphanages lack opportunities to learn traditional roles and skills – many young people emerge from childhood in an institution with no perception of different adult roles, and no understanding of the customs and traditions that underpin daily life.
- Orphanages create a deep-rooted sense of dependency, with children being denied opportunities to learn to become self-reliant and self-directing.
- Children in orphanages often lose their sense of family, clanship or tribal identity; they lack the security and strength that comes from identifying with family and ancestors. Instead, they may assume a negative identity (for example, 'the orphanage child') and face the stigma and prejudice that results.
- Where children have lost contact with their families they will have to enter adult life without the support that the extended family and community traditionally offers in most cultures.[39]

David Tolfree's summary made sense to me. George Mueller would be turning in his grave, I mused. But I knew that, despite all the negative effects of orphanage care, children could be incredibly resilient. By God's grace, children emerge from the most difficult circumstances and make something of themselves.

And I also felt that the flaws in the orphanage model did not take away from the incredible compassion and sacrifice that many missionaries and Christians throughout history, such as George Mueller,[40] had shown in setting up orphanages and caring for orphans. But I was determined to find a better model.

A Mother Substitute

It was an upper-class Englishman who died ten years before I even arrived in Cambodia who held the key to my epiphany. John Bowlby (1907-90) has been described as a genius and one of the three or four most important psychiatrists of the twentieth century. Every student of psychology or psychiatry, and many of a number of other disciplines, would have heard of his watershed work on separation, loss and mourning. Perhaps more than any other figure in recent decades, Bowlby has had profound influence over the treatment of bereaved and separated children in the Western world. And as I read his words, I recognized echoes of his observations about maternal separation in the orphaned kids I knew.

His lifelong work and passion about children separated from their mothers was greatly informed by the trauma he suffered as a child growing up in England. The fourth of six children, John was raised by a nanny in traditional English fashion. He would see his mother for just an hour each day after tea, during which time she would read to him. When John was just four years old, his beloved nanny, who he described as his primary caregiver, left the family. He later wrote that, 'for a child to be looked after entirely by a loving nanny and then for her to leave when he is two or three, or even four or five, can be almost as tragic as the loss of a mother.'[41]

Bowlby said that his mother 'held the view that it was dangerous to spoil children so her responses to bids for attention and affection were the opposite of what was required.' Finally, in another traumatic shock, his father went off to war and John, aged seven, was sent to boarding school, supposedly for his own safety. He later told his wife that he 'would not send even a dog away from home at that age.'

In later life, John Bowlby became a celebrated psychoanalyst and developmental psychologist. He authored more than 150 publications including his famous trilogy: *Separation* (1969), *Attachment* (1973) and *Loss* (1980) which had so much influence on the treatment of orphans and eventually contributed to the widespread abandonment of orphanages in the West.

In 1951, the World Health Organization asked Bowlby to review the impact on children of separation from their parents and caregivers during the Second World War. The resulting study has been translated into fourteen languages and has had an enormous impact on our understanding of care for orphans today.

Bowlby was convinced that an ongoing nurturing relationship between an adult and a young child is as crucial to the child's survival and healthy development as the provision of food, shelter, stimulation and discipline.[42] He came to recognize that the lack of nurture from a mother or mother substitute during childhood could have a devastating effect on the child's health, growth, personality adjustment and cognitive capacity.

I thought about my numerous visits to Cambodian orphanages and realized with a shock that Bowlby had put his finger on what was wrong. As soon as I arrived, the children would crowd around, hungry for my attention. The attention of a complete stranger. Younger ones would cling to my legs and look up at me endearingly, silently imploring me to give them the nurture and love they desperately needed. At the time I thought their indiscriminate attachment and friendliness, clinging and attention-seeking conduct was cute, but it brought tears to my eyes now, as I understood in hindsight that these orphanage children were desperately undernourished, not necessarily for food, but starving for an adult's love and attention. The idea of forty or more kids competing for the affections of a handful of staff deeply disturbed me.

I wondered if Bowlby's insights could be used to redeem the orphanage model. What if enough 'mother substitutes' were employed by the orphanage to provide that love and nurture and attention. I discovered it had been tried before. Two famous child psychologists, Freud and Burlingham, assisted at a home for displaced children and wrote up their experiences.[43] The psychologists were aware of the importance of mother substitute figures and tried to divide the children into very small groups of just three to five children for each caregiver. A very high standard of hygiene and nutrition was provided thanks to a US government grant. Unfortunately, children in the small groups reacted with possessiveness towards the nurses providing care and when nurses had to leave for various reasons, the resulting separation seemed to be just as distressing as the initial separation from the mother. This case study highlighted to me the common difficulty with those institutions that attempt to replicate the family environment by employing staff as mother substitutes. Staff will invariably move on, causing further separation distress to the children in their care. Higher staff turnover meant greater trauma. The same would be true of a succession of foster homes.

In fact, Bowlby maintained that children thrived better in bad homes than in good institutions.

After having my heart for these orphans broken again by Bowlby's insights into their need for a mother substitute, I looked at the UNICEF orphanage data in a new light. One aspect of the data I was particularly interested in examining was the staff to child ratio, which measured how many children are cared for by each staff member.[44]

The orphanages surveyed in Cambodia ranged from twelve to forty-four kids per staff member. Bowlby would have been as shocked as I was. No child, competing with between twelve and forty-four others, could possibly have their needs for individual adult attention and a nurturing mother substitute met under those circumstances. More than half of these orphanage staff were working between seven and eight hours a day.[45] Just 3 per cent were available to the children twenty-four hours a day, as a mother or 'mother substitute' would normally be.

The other aspect of the data I wanted to scrutinize was staff turnover. After all, I figured that staff turnover would give me a sense of how often these children were being separated from subsequent caregivers, further contributing to the difficulty of a 'mother substitute' figure being established in their lives. Of about one hundred orphanages surveyed, I counted ninety-seven staff members who had stopped work in the past twelve months and 226 who had started work in the same time period.[46] Moving to another job, often higher paid, was the most common reason given. Other reasons given indicated that the staff had been terminated by their employer for reasons such as poor performance, breaking the rules, abusing or hitting the children, stealing or corruption. Hardly a stable environment.

I was fast coming to the conclusion that maybe the whole orphanage idea wasn't so great after all. In fact, my experience living amongst the urban poor in Cambodia and working to see those communities transformed was giving me a few more ideas about the pitfalls of orphanages as well.

Firstly, from an economic perspective, it seemed to me that the cost of supporting a child in an orphanage was awfully high. Initially, you had the building costs and then the maintenance costs and ongoing running costs.[47] Once you had a building, your facilities were limited by the constraints of building size and staff numbers. Orphanages for 77,000 Cambodian orphans simply cannot be built and sustained, let alone for 14 million orphans worldwide.

The piles of cash required even to build and run one orphanage would have to be sourced from outside the country, reducing sustainability and increasing dependency on outside funding. That concerned me greatly because starting with the resources of the community is one of the cornerstones of Servants ministry. Sometimes people would say to me 'These people are poor! We just want to bless them.' And I agree wholeheartedly that the rich should be helping the poor, but even Jesus was big on the participation of the poor themselves. In fact, he demonstrated that the poor are not exempt from giving in his observations of the widow and her two mites, and the little boy with nothing but a couple of fish and some bread. If there was one thing I had learned to live by in the slums of Phnom Penh, it was the classic dictum, 'Never do for someone what they can do for themselves.' I saw Westerners, particularly short-term teams, repeatedly ignoring this principle as they arrived in town for two weeks to build and paint churches and schools, taking away from poor Cambodians the one thing they have to contribute, the sweat of their brow. Denying them the dignity of helping themselves.

I looked at the kids at Victory Creek Bridge and beyond, some who had already lost parents, and the thought of removing them from their support network of friends, family and neighbours, even in a slum, truly disturbed me. In the community, children were more likely to be able to stay together with their siblings, a tremendous source of solace and support, and maintain a sense of connectedness with their extended family, their neighbours, their childhood friends, their culture, their heritage and their land.

Looking back at the UNICEF data I was saddened to see that almost half of children in orphanages in Cambodia were actually admitted by parents or relatives, indicating that these children still had family. My heart broke over the thought of a distraught child being dropped off at an orphanage by their own flesh and blood. What would this do to a child's sense of rootedness and connection to kin? What would it do to their self-esteem? One orphanage in Cambodia was compounding the damage by requiring the children to speak only English.[48] Their hearts were in the right place, they wanted the kids to become fluent in English so they could go to America for their university studies. But linguists and anthropologists alike agree that language and culture are intricately linked, and to deny a child the right to speak their own language at home is to deny them an essential link with their cultural heritage.

It dawned on me that children taken out of their communities were being raised in situations that would not prepare them for life as an adult. Living in the cloistered environment of an orphanage could not possibly prepare orphans for adulthood in the community. In other words, institutionalization stores up problems for society, which is ill equipped to cope with an influx of young adults who have not been socialized in the community in which they will have to live.

Visiting orphanages, I realized that the difficulty partly arises because children in orphanages are subject to the routines, procedures and administrative needs of the institution, serving the needs of the home for order, efficiency and conformity. There is an almost complete loss of independence. This is in stark contrast to the normal patterns within a family home and causes serious problems when reintegration into society becomes necessary. In short, children in orphanage care are deprived of the life skills that they would learn growing up in a family and could find it very hard to cope with life outside the institution.[49]

Another problem I saw was that in Cambodia, like in most of the developing world, legal protection for minors is largely unavailable. Children taken from their communities could lose their rights to their parents' house, land and inheritance. Sent away from their village, orphans would be in danger of losing their meagre inheritance: parents' land and other property as well as their sense of belonging to a family.[50]

And lastly, what about abuse in orphanages? Clearly abuse can and does occur in any situation, not just in orphanages. Biological parents and extended family are all potential abusers. But is there anything inherently worse or more dangerous about abuse that occurs in an orphanage? After a lot of study and observation, I came to believe so. Story after story of abuse in residential facilities was whispered to me, and it seemed that Christian church or missionary-run homes were not exempt. Few outsiders are aware or care what takes place inside the walls of these facilities. And as a result, many more situations of abuse in orphanages go unreported and undetected. Kids abused in institutions may well have much greater difficulty in reporting the abuse, escaping from the situation, or getting support from outsiders. Staff prone to abusing have access to a much greater number of vulnerable children. Because these children are utterly dependent on the orphanage, the abuse may continue for a long time. Children with disabilities are especially vulnerable.[51] A survey carried out amongst orphanages in Cambodia found that the vast majority do not do background checks or even require references when employing new staff.[52]

When children in orphanages are subject to physical, sexual or emotional abuse by staff or older children, there are often no established child protection services to ensure a child's safety or prevent future abuse to other children.

I was thoroughly and utterly convinced. An orphanage was definitely not the way to go for the orphan kids I was in contact with. But what other options were out there? My journey was just beginning.

The Birth of Project HALO

The surroundings were far from promising. The Bassac River was a broad brown sewer, its banks lined by a ragged slum that was home to several thousand families.

My Cambodian friend and colleague, Mr Oree, took me down a narrow lane that led to an even narrower one, then to a cluster of homes piled close together. Rough planks and corrugated iron sheets were the building materials of choice. Noisy children charged past me, men sat in doorways.

I was introduced to the boy. Thirteen-year-old Savouen's eyes were sad and downcast, but he was now the man of the house and clearly protective of his younger sister, Layak. Mr Oree had taken care of the kids' mother when she was dying of AIDS, bringing medicine and simple prayers to Jesus for comfort and strength to her bedside. Now the children had lost both parents, and their grandmother, Sally, was looking after them.

Her eyes filling with tears, Sally told me that Savouen and Layak spent hours each day scavenging cans and bottles to recycle to earn money for their school fees. She clearly cared for her grandchildren deeply, but the strain of keeping them in school was becoming too much. She wondered about putting them in an orphanage.

Despite the proliferation of orphanages, 'kinship care', the traditional situation where relatives take in an orphaned child and provide care and support, is still by far the most common way of caring for orphans in Cambodia. Through the centuries, grandmothers like Sally have always been involved in a variety of different ways in the care of children in Cambodia. But the AIDS epidemic has unexpectedly increased the burden on Cambodian grandparents.

There is no old-age pension in Cambodia, nor any other kind of welfare assistance available from the government. In cases where vulnerable older people do not have family to take care of them, they are often seen homeless and begging on the streets.

Older caregivers like Sally struggle with the normal sicknesses and low energy levels of old age. It's hard to go back to work to scrounge an income to support the family especially when her income earning capacity was further compromised by the necessity of caring for children.

The distress and stigma of losing her daughter and son-in-law to AIDS brought feelings of isolation for Sally, and by the time I met her she was really struggling. She grasped my arm with the leathery skin of her bony fingers and begged me to help.

In my visits around the slums I was struck by the fact that there are old folk like Sally all over Cambodia who display remarkable resilience and play an extremely important role in the care of their grandchildren orphaned by AIDS. It is an often overlooked fact that this is a reciprocal relationship where the grandkids grow up and provide their grandparents with economic security and emotional and psychosocial support and in return grandparents provide a loving home with care and emotional support when the orphaned children are younger.[53] These grandparents are the knowledge-bearers of Cambodian society and are an important educational influence in the lives of thousands of Cambodian orphans.

I realized that there was no ideal solution to the problem of orphanhood, since nothing and no one can truly replace a mother and father, only better or worse alternatives. Apart from going to live in an orphanage, which I had concluded was less than ideal, the options for orphaned kids in Cambodia were fairly limited. Cambodian communities, despite decades of war and societal breakdown, had already absorbed thousands of orphans into the extended family and informal community systems. At least five per cent of families nationwide had taken in children who were not their own. However, only one in twenty of these families received any kind of outside support at all.[54] Households headed by elderly people and women would especially struggle. Already living at the edge of poverty, they would have to stretch their insufficient resources even further to care for orphaned relatives. Child-headed and teenager-headed households also battled to survive, dependent on each other and particularly on older siblings. Families like Sally's were buckling under the burden.

Nay and I sat down again to pray and talk about what God might be calling us to do for Savouen, Layak, Visal and other friends and neighbours who were affected by AIDS. Starting an orphanage was out of the question, though we were still inspired by George Mueller's dependence on prayer for the orphans. We knew we somehow wanted to work arm in arm with local Christians, encouraging and inspiring them to become involved with the orphans in their own communities. The rest of the Servants team had lots of ideas too and so Nay began to sketch out on paper what a ministry to help these families might look like. I came up with the acronym, HALO, for the project name. It stood for Hope, Assistance and Love for Orphans. I wanted the Hope to signify the spiritual needs of the orphans, the Assistance to refer to their physical needs for food, clothing and shelter, and the Love to denote their emotional and social needs. And so, one sweaty night in a tiny Phnom Penh slum house, Project HALO was born.

Our vision was to see Cambodian communities, led by the church, caring for their own orphans. We had no idea what it would become.

A natural place to start was with the HIV positive people already being cared for through the Servants AIDS homecare project. At the time they were ministering to about three hundred people, many with full-blown AIDS.

We began to accompany Mr Oree and our neighbour Sareem on their visits through the slums and squatter settlements along the river with a new sense of purpose. We found that the majority of these patients were also parents, some with as many as ten children. We sat in their homes and held their hands. We listened and prayed with them. We talked and played with their children. We collected information and took photos of the parents, information and photos that would become invaluable to their children in later years.

At the same time, we began to think about how to care for these children after their parents died. One Sunday, I got up in the little Khmer church we were attending, the church that had seen Visal live out his short and painful life and eventually die. I spoke of the plight of these children. I pointed out biblical injunctions to care for widows and orphans and then I gave an impassioned plea for foster parents, mother substitutes for these orphans. 'Our neighbours are dying of AIDS and their children are being orphaned. Who will help these children who have no one?' I asked only partly rhetorically. 'Who will be the hands and feet of Jesus in serving these orphans?' Afterwards I took names of people who were interested in informally adopting orphans and we announced an upcoming training course for those who wanted to learn and know more. Through our network of Cambodian colleagues and volunteers, more people signed up and within the space of a couple of months we were ready to run a training course for potential foster parents with several dozen participants.

At the first session, we talked about the statistics for orphaning in Cambodia, we talked about the children we knew personally who were being orphaned in our slum communities and we talked about what a Christian response might be. I knew that I should restate the unpaid nature of this work, since I was aware that many with good hearts but empty pockets were interested in the financial benefits of the ministry. The next week, numbers were down and I knew that those who were looking to be paid were gone. Week after week we sat in the church hall, discussing the nutritional needs of the children, ways to treat minor illnesses, schooling options and other logistics.

One of their major concerns was potential infection with the HIV virus. For many it was a revelation that not all children of parents with AIDS would be HIV positive themselves. Mrs Neang, the heavy Cambodian woman who ran our Servants nutrition clinic, came in and shared about the children she was treating on a daily basis. Pinching the flesh of her ample stomach, she started with a joke about how if anyone should know about being well nourished, it was her. Nodding their heads with new-found respect, the group laughed warmly. Mrs Neang went on to explain about the babies born to HIV positive mothers.

'Listen to me!' She pressed home the point with her chubby index finger. 'Only one in three babies born to an HIV positive mother is going to have picked up the virus. And if we can give Mum the antiretroviral drugs she needs during the birthing process, then her baby has less than a one in ten chance of becoming positive – especially if Mum doesn't breastfeed.'

The group nodded sagely, as it sank in that the majority of children orphaned by AIDS were in perfect health. Mrs Neang's talk relieved a lot of fears and people began to ask me when they could have their kids. I explained to them that we still needed to go through the interview and screening process.

One of the church elders, a lady I called Aunty Lin (name changed for privacy), had really impressed me throughout the training course. She asked insightful questions, spoke passionately on behalf of the children and had the respect of the other participants, so I asked her to help me conduct the screening interviews. I figured she would have a better cultural grasp of the situation than I could ever have and, frankly, I needed her wisdom. Aunty Lin and I began visiting the homes of the potential foster parents. We were assessing the homes and families for suitability, trying to ascertain the motivations of the potential foster parents.

After one interview, Aunty Lin took me aside and asked if I had noticed the type of children the family had asked for. I nodded in agreement. I had perceived something not quite right too.

'I think they want a twelve-year-old girl because they need someone to do housework and help in their shop. I don't think they are suitable.'

I was pleased with Aunty Lin's wisdom. She was able to give balanced assessments on each family that rang true. By the end of the interviews we had whittled down the original crowd of willing foster parents to a healthy bunch of good families. I was pleased with Aunty Lin's work and I asked her to continue helping me with Project HALO.

Aunty Lin was a widow, the mother of five polite teenage children and chief source of support for two nephews, a young unmarried brother and her elderly parents. She had financial pressures that would one day be her undoing. Together they all lived in a wooden house about five hundred metres from our own home at Victory Creek Bridge. Because she was supporting a large household, we couldn't take her away from her usual activities and expect her to work in Project HALO full time without some alternative source of income. So we sat down together and worked out a proper work contract, which included a small salary that would help meet her household responsibilities. Aunty Lin had originally signed up for the foster parents training course with the idea of voluntarily taking in a couple of orphans herself. But I was realizing that God was going to take this sacrificial response and build on it, adding blessing to faithfulness.

Nay was busy too, day by day, visiting the HIV positive parents and collecting information on their circumstances. We desperately needed to get reluctant parents to think about their children's care after they died. Often no plans were made and the children were being suddenly orphaned with no idea of the wishes of the parents. Because of deeply held superstitions about the discussion of death, many were hesitant to talk about the future orphanhood of their children for fear that they might hasten its arrival. We learned to ask tactfully around the issue, 'If you were not around, who would care for your children?' Almost invariably, the response would be 'I want my children to live in the Servants orphanage!' We recognized again the unwavering and widespread belief in orphanages as a wonderful place for children to grow up.

'We don't have an orphanage. Do you have a Plan B? Don't the children have a grandmother or an aunty or any other relatives?' We would inquire innocently, knowing full well they would have. 'Oh yes. But they are so poor. They couldn't possibly take care of my children.' Sometimes, the parents even attempted to hide the existence of relatives, believing that they would therefore be more likely to get their children into our non-existent orphanage. We became adept at asking the right questions, going after important information in creative ways. For example, after a while, instead of asking 'Do you have any relatives?' which might elicit a negative response, we began asking 'So, do your relatives live in this village or the next one?' or 'What does your sister do for a living?' If we were off the mark, they would simply tell us they didn't have a sister. But more often than not, we were able to get to the truth without having to wade through a shoal of red herrings.

Our research and experience was showing that in fact, extended families were playing a major role in caring for Cambodian orphans. After grandmothers, the second major category providing care to orphans in Cambodia were aunts and uncles. These people, mainly women, were often caring for their own biological children as well. A common criticism of this situation was that the orphaned children were not treated equally in the household. While most instances of kinship care were clearly situations where the children were receiving love, care and nurturing from the extended family, other anecdotal information suggested the possibility of exploitation and abuse by relatives in a small percentage of cases.[55]

We recognized that an unmonitored placement with extended family might turn out to be not in the best interests of the child and careful monitoring and follow-up quickly became a cornerstone of Project HALO's approach. What was certain was that the addition of extra children in any household placed strain on the resources of that family and would result in more economic and psychosocial pressure.

Aunty Lin began accompanying us on the visits to families and she added her earthy wisdom to every situation. She would cajole and wheedle crucial information that we had no hope of obtaining. Her casual chats with neighbours and various family members helped to build up a picture of the true situation facing each family. She was adept at becoming just another aunty in each household. Seated on the wooden floor of a shack, legs tucked beneath her to one side in traditional Khmer style, she would spend time just plaiting a girl's tresses or picking nits out of a boy's hair. All the while she would be helping the family work through the major issues they were facing. Oftentimes she would encourage a family to come to church: 'They care about you at church. It's like a whole new family that can help you out when times are tough,' she would explain patiently. And very often they came. Other times she would share with orphaned children about their Father God in heaven, who would never leave them or forsake them.

Aunty Lin was doing fine, but all was not well between Nay and I.

Plates in a Basket will Rattle

Nay and I were finding working together to be a major challenge. On top of the stress of seeing desperately sad and frustrating situations on a daily basis, we were then returning together to our tiny home at Victory Creek Bridge at the end of the day. There was no escape from each other.

With just a handful of years of marriage under our belt at that stage, we were still learning what it meant to share our lives with the other person. In fact we were still discovering who the other person was. We had earlier got hold of a great book about the five love languages and another about personality types and with no television to distract us in the evenings we spent long hours discussing our differences. On almost every point we were exact opposites. Where I thrived on verbal encouragement and praise, Nay was suspicious of mere words, and unmotivated to express approval. Nay blossomed from spending quality time together, while I was task oriented and bored by sitting around navel-gazing.

During the day, we were supposedly co-leaders of the project. But we both had strong and sometimes incompatible ideas on how to progress the ministry. For example, Nay had designed a simple paper-based system to keep track of the family data, which I saw could quickly accumulate into unmanageable piles. As a surprise, I spent several evenings designing an attractive and user-friendly database on our laptop computer, which I proudly unveiled with a flourish one night. To my dismay, Nay was silent, brooding. Seeing the verbal approval I had anticipated slipping through my fingers, I clenched my teeth and said 'What's wrong?' 'I've already designed a paper-based system to hold all this data. I don't want it all on a computer. What if it crashes? You haven't included all the information I wanted!'

I pleaded, I persuaded, I argued and I raged but there was no convincing her and the conversation deteriorated into an exchange of bitter recriminations. We spent the night lying frostily with backs to each other. Needless to say we were heading for a showdown.

One of the problems was that we were too often taking our clashes over procedures or disagreements over ministry decisions home with us. And as a result, we were treating our neighbours to some raging arguments. In these spats, I preferred to keep my voice down and discuss things heatedly but with a certain amount of control. Nay preferred to scream and shout, letting it all out, in what I wrongly perceived to be an uncontrolled display of unnecessary hysteria. I was worried that our witness in our community would be compromised; after all, there is no such thing as a private heated discussion in a slum community.

But over time I realized that being real and authentic about our struggles in our community was actually not so bad. As a friend of mine put it, living in the slum it's impossible to do a quick change from Clark Kent to Superman to gratify our spiritual egos every time we go out of the door 'to do ministry'. Curiously, when we allowed people to see that we are human, our Christianity appeared less remote and therefore more accessible, more viable, for them. They began to see it doesn't take a saint to live a Christian life.

But one night, Nay and I disagreed over something that I can no longer recall, and it turned into a serious dispute. Nay was crying and I was very angry. With a slam of the door she was gone. It was about eleven o'clock at night and my anger quickly dissipated as I worried about her safety on the streets at this late hour. By the time I had rushed down the steps after her, she was gone, having jumped on a nearby motorbike taxi and sped off, tears streaming down her face. I sat upstairs, alternately fretting about her and cursing her stupidity. The thoughts bouncing around madly in my head were of packing it all in, getting away, escape. I felt like a complete failure. It was a long, dark, wearying night, but with the morning light came fresh perspective. Nay came in the door a while later and we embraced.

'Where were you?' I implored.

'Oh, I just got a room at a cheap hotel downtown.'

We were certainly no saints but our Cambodian neighbours were not fazed at all. They just smiled understandingly and murmured, 'Plates in a basket will rattle.' The ancient Khmer proverb was spot on, and ours was a very small basket. They witnessed our spats and we witnessed their domestic disputes, which often turned violent.

To make matters worse, Nay's experience of being a missionary in Cambodia was markedly different from my own. When Nay was growing up there was always a sense in which God's call on her life to serve her own people was a call to go home. But once in Cambodia she quickly realized that Cambodia wasn't home. There was a sense of familiarity about it but it was certainly not home. Which left her wondering, where then was home? Where did she fit?

This was all compounded by the fact that being Chinese Cambodian, she doesn't have the same features as most Cambodians and is most commonly mistaken for Japanese or Korean. So, at times she was accepted as Cambodian but more often she was seen as a foreigner. Having spent so much time in New Zealand, Nay's Khmer language was pretty rusty, and she never quite regained the fluency needed to convince people she was a local.

Adding insult to injury, women in Cambodia have historically been strong – stronger than many other Asian countries – but it is still a highly patriarchal society. To our annoyance, I was often treated with deference while Nay would be completely ignored. Typical would be our entrance into a new church. The pastor would come running over to me, greeting me effusively, while completely disregarding Nay's presence beside me. During the service, there would be an official welcome made to the white foreigner, no mention of Nay. Nay put up with this unbalanced situation heroically, rarely saying anything. But I knew it got her down and it bugged me a lot that she was constantly undervalued in this way.

Something had to come to a head and Nay and I realized we needed to get outside help to work through some of the issues we were facing. We quietly sought out a professional counsellor and went along for several sessions that were reasonably helpful. Probably the most valuable insight was that working together in a very stressful ministry and living together in cramped conditions was simply unsustainable. It was clearly time for some changes. Nay decided to leave Project HALO leadership to me and Aunty Lin.

The change made a huge difference as we realized that Nay had also been deeply psychologically and emotionally affected by the frustrating situations of the families in the AIDS homecare project. Their grindingly depressing circumstances, combined with the constant battling on behalf of the children, was proving to be too much of a strain. As soon as she stopped regularly visiting these families, she began to emerge once again as the cheerful, positive woman I had once known. Ironically, Nay plunged herself into an equally depressing ministry, but this time it seemed to energize her.

Gold and Cloth

Nay began going along to the local brothel each week where Dr Janet Cornwall and Mrs Sokum, one of our Cambodian Christian co-workers, held a clinic for about eighty women trapped in commercial sex work. The brothel was really just another slum alley. Kids and dogs played outside in the muddy lane while inside, small rooms were being used for the sex trade. Nay began to get alongside the girls of this alley and quickly established an intimate rapport with them. She looked forward to the brothel clinic each week and took a course in treating sexually transmitted infections[56] so she could help medically. Many nights we would lie in bed and Nay would tell me about the girls she was befriending. Unseen in the dark, silent tears would roll down my cheeks as my heart broke over the girls and their stories. At times I had to ask her to stop, unable to bear any more of their heartache.

One night, Nay told me about eighteen-year-old Ret, who had just arrived in the brothel, fresh faced and innocent. She had come from the countryside, dispatched by her poor and indebted family to find work in one of the factories and send home desperately needed money. But getting a job in one of the local garment factories meant the usual payments to guards and supervisors. Ret couldn't afford the $30 she would need to get in. After weeks of depleting her meagre savings to nothing she faced a horrible decision, return to her starving and indebted family, empty-handed and having used their only resources to come to the city and fail miserably, or take the only work available, as a commercial sex worker. Ret saw no other way out and when a friend introduced her to the brothel, she swore she would just work a few days to get enough money to pay back her family's debts and then return home. But like the other 70,000 prostitutes who work all over Cambodia, she found it a difficult situation to escape. The brothel owner quickly made sure that Ret became indebted to her for rent and upkeep. Then there were the local police to be paid off each month, another debt the brothel owner added to her tab. And the income from selling her body to drunks and thugs, less than the price of a can of beer for a session, proved not as lucrative as she had hoped. Within days, Ret's complexion was blotchy, her energy was low and the life was gone from her eyes. She had already served a couple of dozen customers, but was no longer counting.

Nay worked hard to convince girls like Ret to leave the brothel, especially when they first arrived since they quickly grew jaded and psychologically trapped. One day Ret confided in Nay that she couldn't face living in the brothel another day. She was fearful of contracting AIDS, having seen so many of her friends succumb to the disease, and the grinding cycle of selling her body to be used and abused night and day had taken its toll on her health and emotional stability. Nay and Janet arranged to meet her outside the brothel the following day.

The next day, with a furtive glance over her shoulder at the brothel alley that had been her home for several months, Ret jumped on a waiting motorbike taxi with Janet and they sped off to a safe house. On arrival, Ret looked up doubtfully at the huge, quiet building, unsure of herself and the decision she had made. It was a far cry from the lively slum alley she was now used to living in.

Later, when Ret ran away from the safe house and returned to the brothel, Nay would ask herself guiltily if there was anything she could have done differently to change the final outcome. A Christian safe house for at-risk girls was newly opened over the river and became available as an alternative to the destructive lifestyle in the brothel. They offered vocational training courses and a small monthly stipend. Nay decided that she should go and work part-time in the new safe house as well, to follow up girls like Ret who came out of the brothel.

Over the next few months and years though, others did leave and they left for good. It was these girls that kept Nay going.

One of the regular features of the brothel clinic was the distribution of condoms to the girls. We all figured that saving people's lives was consistent with our Christian convictions, especially under these circumstances where the women were so powerless and trapped for economic or social reasons. The normal route of HIV infection in Cambodia is from commercial sex worker to husband to wife to newborn baby. We wanted to break that vicious cycle, that was resulting in thousands of deaths and thousands more orphans. We did this not just by encouraging the women in the brothel to use condoms, but by doing outreach education amongst high risk groups such as motorbike taxi guys and unemployed young men, warning them of the consequences of their actions and correcting some of the unhelpful myths about HIV and AIDS. For example, it was believed by many that if someone looks healthy, they couldn't possibly be HIV positive. Men, like gold, do not tarnish, while women, like cloth, once stained are ruined for life.

Teaching the easy to remember *A for abstinence before marriage, B for Be faithful to your spouse, and C for use Condoms if you can't do A and B*, we took the ABC message into the snooker halls, bars, cafés and street hangouts of the slums. It is a controversial, yet effective message being promoted by Christian groups all over the world wherever AIDS is rampant.

At times, however, we were accused of compromising the gospel. Some felt Servants should be preaching loudly against sin in the brothels and refusing to allow the use of lifesaving condoms since this was supposedly tantamount to condoning or even encouraging sin. If I could, I would invite these people to meet some of the girls in our alleyway, to hear their stories, to see their entrapment and then decide whether they would deny them a condom to keep them alive just a little longer, while we tried to find a way out for them. I would invite them to look into the eyes of the eight children in one family who were now orphaned because their father got drunk one night and visited a prostitute and then brought the deadly disease home to his innocent wife. I would invite them to tell those children that given the choice they would have denied their father a condom, because he deserved to die.

One day, I was asked to host a very prominent American evangelist who was visiting Phnom Penh and wanted to see firsthand some of the Servants ministry. My first clue that we were going to have trouble was when he refused to remove his cowboy boots to enter the tiny home of one of our AIDS patients. In Cambodian culture it is very rude to wear your shoes inside someone else's house, but my gentle suggestions were brushed aside.

Before the meeting, I had been warned of his anti-condom stance by some of his colleagues and I was a little hesitant to go ahead. But they assured me he would be open to hearing our point of view, since we were truly working at the coalface. Unfortunately, his visit coincided with the International AIDS conference in Thailand and the television news was full of AIDS activists prancing around in condom hats and designer clothing made entirely from condoms promoting the idea that these rubber sheathes were the only solution to the AIDS epidemic spreading around the world.

I began to sense that Cowboy Boots was in a cantankerous mood. He kept making comments about the activists and expressing his incredulity that so-called liberal Christians were jumping on the 'condom bandwagon'. Finally, I could take it no longer and I blurted out, 'Actually sir, WE are evangelicals but we have decided that giving out condoms in certain situations is entirely consistent with our Christian belief in the sanctity of life. After all, if we all got what we deserve for our sin, there wouldn't be very many of us left, would there, sir?'

Well, that did it. He turned to me with a steely look in his eye and growled, 'I suppose you think Jesus would be standing on street corners handing out condoms? What would Jesus do? Jesus wasn't interested in saving people's physical bodies; he died on the cross and rose again to save people's souls. THAT is the gospel and nothing more.'

I mustered all my courage and looked him straight in the eye, trying to ignore the fact that the man was a world-famous evangelist and highly respected Christian leader. 'Sir, if your own daughter was forced into prostitution, wouldn't you want a bunch of caring Christians to come and minister to her with God's grace, giving her condoms to keep her alive until they were able to get her out of the brothel?'

I could almost see the steam coming out of his ears, as he physically swallowed his anger. He stared at me trying to figure out who this young upstart was, then with a wave of his hand, he wrote me off with a patronizing drawl, 'You listen here. I've got a few years on you, sonny boy."

And that was the end of it. My adrenalin was running high but I figured I'd said enough. I heard later that I had provoked quite a controversy amongst his inner circle, a real storm in a teacup, and though I felt battered, I was glad I had said what I did. After all, it is a life and death situation for the girls of that brothel and the families we were working with every day, not just a minor theological disagreement. Cowboy Boots could think what he liked, I was the one who would have to look into their eyes and walk with them through their pain, not the armchair critics.

Nay wasn't in the least bit fazed by any of the controversy and she continued to live out the gospel of grace amongst those girls for quite some time to come. But more change was afoot, in our community and in our family.

The End of the Road

Grasping the photocopied papers, our neighbours at Victory Creek Bridge stood around shocked, gossiping soberly about the impending eviction. For years it had been rumoured that the Cambodian government had plans to turn our little sewage creek into a major sewer canal and now time had finally run out. Those who owned the land near the creek were given alternative plots of land outside the city, which they promptly sold to speculators for a handful of dollars. Those of us who were renting were given no compensation and left to find other affordable housing in the city, typically in another slum community. We lived just a couple of feet outside the eviction zone, but with a major sewage channel being built and most of our friends gone, the community just didn't feel the same.

At the same time, Nay was seven months pregnant with our first child and after three years at Victory Creek Bridge we sensed God was moving us on. With tears we all said goodbye: our friends and neighbours to embark on an uncertain future, Nay and I to New Zealand for the big event.

Our son was born back in New Zealand after three days of labour. A big boy, over nine pounds, Nay was far too small to push him out. Finally, the doctors decided to perform an emergency caesarean section. The birth problems quickly faded from our minds as we focused on our newborn baby. We had already decided to name him Jayden* in memory of Nay's father, Jayu. We were also excited to find the name in the book of Nehemiah, in a list of the builders of Nehemiah's wall, and especially liked the Hebrew meaning, 'God hears'. For us his multilayered name reminded us that God has heard the cry of the poor. After a few months with Jayden's grandparents, we returned to Cambodia and began to search for a new slum community.

The slum at the End of the Road originally sprang up around three imposing apartment blocks. Once elegant, they were built by the government in the 1950s for airforce pilots and their families. In the mid 1970s, when the Khmer Rouge evacuated everyone out of town, the blocks stood crumbling, empty and decaying. In 1979, after the Vietnamese overthrow of the Khmer Rouge, people poured back into town, grabbing whatever house they could. In a bizarre free-for-all, those with muscle took the biggest mansions, while those with no access to guns or clout took the riverside shacks in the empty derelict slums. No one, rich or poor, had land titles in those days.

Because the End of the Road was near the electricity company, it was quickly swamped with electricity workers and their families. Before long, slum shacks began springing up on the land around the apartments. With no garbage collection system in place the land became littered with a layer of trash, now a two metre

---

* Nehemiah 3:7 – but it's spelt as Jadon.

deep cesspit crawling with rats and covering the area of a football field between the two buildings.

One day, venturing down a shadowy and crumbling concrete alley, I happened upon the End of the Road community. Asking around, I located an available apartment on the ground floor and within a few days we had moved in with paintbrushes and cleaning equipment. In bygone days it might once have been described as having character, even a certain charm, but by the time we moved in, it was more than ready for demolition.

The room containing a filthy squat toilet was a black hole. The doorway was guarded by a barricade of spiders' webs and it had long since been abandoned to the rats and cockroaches. The bathroom was not much better. But along with the rest of the team and some other friends we managed to clean it up enough to move in. In the living room, one wall was taken up with huge wooden shutters which I eventually managed to prise open. Opening them out wide I marvelled at the view. Ramshackle slum shacks built to within inches of our window and a field of garbage were the main sight, but the air flow was good and it was nice to have so much light in our living quarters.

That evening we were sitting on the floor under the open windows, exhausted after a day of painting and cleaning. Suddenly, a huge watery whooshing sound accompanied the splatter of an unidentified liquid all over our heads and shoulders. Furious, I leapt to my feet and looked outside to find the source of the spray. But there was nothing except a few plump rats. Then, twisting my head up, I examined the huge wooden window shutters and realized that the apartment above had thrown their waste out of their own window and it had landed on our shutters, which were designed in just such a way as to direct the water straight into our room.

How obnoxious! Over the next few days we saw this repeated often; rubbish and waste water was thrown frequently over our neighbours' tin roofs and onto our shutters from the apartments above. I asked the neighbour in the wooden house in front how he felt about it and he just shook his head in disgust saying, 'I have no words. I have no words.' I knew how he felt, though I had a few choice words I would have used given half the chance. At times, in the middle of the night a discarded coconut husk would land on a tin roof somewhere in our neighbourhood and I would wake with a start, imagining a family somewhere nearby startled into consciousness by an enormous coconut explosion above their sleeping heads.

Our newborn baby son Jayden became an instant celebrity at the End of the Road. We were called '*Mak* Jayden' and '*Pa* Jayden' (Jayden's mum and dad) by everyone right from the beginning. Everywhere we went, Jayden was the centre of attention and the main topic of conversation. One of the first things they all noticed was that he had three crowns or swirls in the back of his hair. This became an object of much fascination since depending who you talk to in Cambodia having three crowns can mean having three wives, being three times as naughty or being three times as prosperous. We hoped it wouldn't be all of these explanations rolled into one! Jayden had retained his birth weight and grown rapidly so that by six months he was a huge butterball. One day, after several days of diarrhoea we worriedly packed him off to the doctor. The doctor reassured us by pointing out that Jayden was in fact a very robust little boy. I had to admit it was true. Jayden was big for his age, particularly compared to the tiny Cambodian kids around our house. He thrived on his mother's milk and when the day came that he began demanding food, he demanded lots of it!

Friends and acquaintances sometimes wondered aloud if it was right for us to take our baby to live in a Cambodian slum. As if we hadn't given it a second thought ourselves! In fact, Nay and I had agonized over the issue, giving it a lot of thought and prayer.

We felt strongly that what Jayden needed wasn't necessarily the comforts and gadgets of the West, but parents who loved him and spent time with him, parents who sought first the kingdom of God, parents who showed what it meant to pursue God rather than career or possessions.

We planned carefully what kind of house and community we would need to find in order to ensure our son's safety. We wanted to avoid a community that flooded, common in Cambodian slums, but dangerous for small children. We wanted a house that we could keep reasonably clean inside, to make sure the conditions were hygienic enough for Jayden. Our apartment at the End of the Road was just right.

Before long we realized that although Jayden was growing up without a lot of the paraphernalia of his peers back home in New Zealand, what he lacked in possessions he more than made up in richness of relationships. Nay and I doted on him, and he was surrounded by neighbourhood friends who were devoted to their little buddy. In particular, Tee, the kid next door, was a gentle-spirited little boy of about seven years old who loved Jayden like a younger sibling.

Jayden's first birthday was a massive party. We began by talking it up for several weeks in advance of the big day. The local kids kept asking, 'Is today Jayden's birthday?' The sense of excitement was growing. Finally the big day arrived and we put on a spread that made the kids' eyes widen with glee. So many people crowded into our tiny home that it was standing room only as we passed around the muffins and played games. What a party!

As Jayden began to speak, his first words were a mixture of Khmer and English. My mum was horrified to hear that his first word was 'butt', until I explained that it was actually a Khmer word meaning gone or lost and he was talking about his beloved ball. Considering he was trying to get his head around two languages, Jayden was a quick speaker and we were excited that he was blessed with the opportunity to grow up bilingual.

One of the toughest challenges we faced raising Jayden at the End of the Road was getting him to sleep through the night. We were keen to try some of the techniques from home that used controlled crying and routines to teach him to go to sleep on his own. The problem was, leaving a child crying without responding is considered cruel in Cambodian culture, especially at night when all the neighbours are trying to sleep. Furthermore, Cambodians all sleep together in one bed, especially when children are younger. Our neighbours were horrified when we decorated our second bedroom with colourful curtains and announced that Jayden would sleep in there. Alone! I heard one Cambodian friend commenting that the reason Westerners have so few children is they don't have enough rooms to isolate them all in. In the end it wasn't an issue, Jayden simply refused to sleep in a room all by himself and screamed the place down if we tried to force him. Out of consideration for our neighbours and to reduce our own stress levels we decided to relax and go with whatever worked for us. In practice that meant sleeping together Cambodian style under one mosquito net. It was a huge relief the first night we did it. No more fighting our way through several layers of mosquito net to get to a crying child, no more worrying that his crying would wake up the neighbours, no more distressed child wanting his mum and dad at night.

Later I came to realize that the Cambodian method of parenting children during their first two or three years is known as Attachment Parenting. The main components of this approach are carrying the baby close to your body a lot, sleeping together in one bed and responding to the cries of the child. It is named after John Bowlby's attachment theory.

Another steep learning curve was in disciplining Jayden. A handful of our neighbours were very tough on their kids. Some beatings would go on for up to an hour, using anything that came to hand: coat hangers, sticks, fists, even threatening with knives. The language used could be just as violent: 'If you don't shut up I'm going to cut your head off', 'stop crying or I'll shoot you'. This really distressed me and I found it difficult to know when and how to intervene. It was a clear societal norm in Cambodian culture that you never interfered in domestic arguments or the child discipline of your neighbours. I became very sensitive to the sound of children crying in the community and would strain my ears to hear whether they were being beaten or not. Several times I couldn't stand it any longer and I would have to go and confront the person.

With Jayden, though we did smack him sometimes, it was almost always after counting slowly to three and we tried hard to develop alternative ways of disciplining him, such as sending him into the corner or out of the room and teaching him to say sorry afterwards.

One day a visitor from New Zealand was praying for us and they asked God to bless Nay in her 'Prophetic Motherhood' role. I smiled at the term, but it struck me that Nay really was showing our neighbours that there were other ways to discipline a child other than beating the living daylights out of them. At the same time, they were also teaching us a lot. Jayden was growing up to be a strong-willed but generally very happy and outgoing boy.

We got lots of advice from our neighbours about child rearing. The food we gave Jayden to eat was a constant source of interest. They claimed he had such a great complexion because he was being reared on rice. In fact, Jayden ate almost anything that was on sale around our community, including the deep-fried garter snakes and frogs sold on sticks as a delicacy. He developed quite a robust constitution and was able to eat a lot of things that would have me running to the toilet soon afterwards.

By this time, we had one of our own and another several hundred orphan kids in Project HALO.

Church Planting Amongst Orphans

Project HALO was expanding rapidly. Geographically, we still concentrated on the slum areas south of our home at the End of the Road on the outskirts of Phnom Penh. But about twenty new children a month were coming into the program. Our original proposal had set the target of reaching fifty children affected by AIDS in the first year but we had surpassed that within a matter of a few weeks. The challenge was not how to go wide, but how to go deep.

One of the advantages of enabling orphans to stay in their own communities was that we were able to minister to entire families, clusters of neighbours and ultimately communities. Our burning desire was to see the orphans' lives, their families' lives and their communities impacted by Christ. But we knew that this kind of total life transformation would take more than simply getting them to make a verbal acknowledgement of Jesus. As exhilarating as it was to help people make a first-time decision for Christ, we learned that such decisions were not always as they first appeared. What would truly count, over time, were thoroughly transformed lives.

We desperately wanted to see these families discover God's agenda for their lives, to help them move from the status quo to becoming the people God created them to be. Accepting Jesus Christ as Lord and Saviour was the most crucial step in that movement but probably not the first or the only step.

I drew Aunty Lin a picture of a long road and populated it with stick people, representing the journey between spiritual deadness and abundant life. Lives shaped by poverty and oppression seldom change very fast, so in Project HALO we tried to appreciate every small step in the right direction on the road to Christ. We learned to celebrate every healthy decision, every spiritual barrier removed, every good new friendship, every lesson learned, every heartfelt prayer, every addiction broken, every useful skill developed, every conflict peacefully resolved, and every righteous moment enjoyed by everyone we knew, and all the more so when we sensed that God had used us to make one of those beautiful things happen.[57] By the grace of God, these were all steps towards growth. So when measuring our impact, we didn't just count first-time decisions or baptisms, we thought about all the other little steps along the way as well in their journey towards Christ.

Grandmother Sally and her two grandchildren, Savouen and Layak, were one of the first families we got to know well and the initially faltering steps they took on their spiritual journey were a real encouragement to me. One day, Sally called us desperately for help, saying Layak was very ill. She had already taken Layak to see the local *kru kmae* and there had been no improvement. Aunty Lin and I felt privileged to be asked to pray for Layak and we encouraged Sally to turn to Jesus for help in times of trial like this. When Layak recovered, Sally seemed more open to Jesus than before and she allowed her grandchildren to begin attending a local church. Over the years, Sally went through many difficult times, including a period where she felt someone had put a curse on her. But slowly and surely, two steps forward, one step back, Sally and her grandchildren moved along in their spiritual journey towards Christ. Her grandson Savouen eventually became a vibrant youth leader in his church and Sally became a committed Christian, volunteering to visit and minister to other families living with AIDS in the Servants homecare program.

Another family and community that underwent a remarkable transformation was located about five hundred metres from our home at the End of the Road, one alley south of the brothel Nay was ministering in. It all started with an energetic woman named Vee and her three daughters. Vee's husband was HIV positive and was already receiving medicine and prayer from our AIDS homecare team. When her husband died, Vee had her final HIV test, which came back negative. Miraculously, she had escaped infection. Aunty Lin got to know Vee and her daughters and began to share about God's grace with them, pointing out that God had helped Vee stay HIV negative. Other neighbours, who had seen Servants volunteers ministering to Vee's husband, began asking questions and before long a small group of seekers was meeting to study the Bible each week in that slum.

On rare occasions we sensed that God was calling us to plant a church, but more often we felt he was calling us to build up local churches and feed new believers into them. In this way we were not seen as a competing group, building our own empire, but as servants and partners with local Christians. This stance allowed us greater influence in a wide variety of churches and resulted in greater partnership possibilities and potential for mass mobilization of Christians than if we were perceived as being solely church planters or empire builders.

So, rather than putting up a Servants sign and planting our own church at Vee's house, we invited another local church to come alongside and run the Bible studies and children's programs that were beginning to take off. It was risky; we were giving them control and empowering them to make the decisions, good and bad. But before long, there was a vibrant worshipping community squeezing into Vee's wooden house every Sunday morning and several nights a week. It was exciting to see them grow into a church.

After a few years, some Korean missionaries built them a huge church building with a tall red steeple rising up from the heart of the slum, which they were all very proud of. Though we wouldn't have planned it that way, and we might have done a few things differently had we been in charge, I still believe we did the right thing in relinquishing control and allowing room for others.

We asked Vee to take in a little girl named Tida who had recently been orphaned and needed a temporary home to live in. Tida thrived amongst her three foster sisters and quickly came to enjoy participating in the church activities. Though she had lost her mother and father to AIDS, she discovered a Father in heaven who loved her very much, and a church family who would accept and nurture her. I remember one day I was visiting Vee's home and Tida was there playing with a little soft toy, a lamb that had once been white but was now dirty brown. It was obviously a beloved plaything. The lamb played the tune, *Jesus loves me* and someone asked Tida if she knew what the tune was. Tida proudly recited, 'Jesus loves me, this I know' in English.

'Yes, but do you know what it means?'

'Of course I do,' retorted Tida, and she repeated the song again word for word, in Khmer this time.

Eventually, Tida's married older sister was able to take her in and Tida left the community to be reunited with her family. But she took with her a new-found strength, a confidence that she would have family wherever she went and a passionate love for her Father in heaven.

Here Come the Jesus People

The first time I met seventeen-year-old Maryanne she was wearing a pink headscarf indicating that she was a Cham.

For most in this nation, to be Cambodian is to be Buddhist. But there is also an ethnic minority called the Cham people, who are traditionally Muslims. Across the river a few miles from our home at the End of the Road, there was a small Cham community living in a bustling riverside slum. Through Project HALO we were able to get to know some of these families and slowly build some relationships in what was historically a very unresponsive community.

As I sat in Maryanne's tiny wooden hut that first meeting, she whispered her heartbreaking story to me. Maryanne's father had walked out on his family a couple of years before, leaving her mother reeling from the shock of being HIV positive and facing the future alone without a breadwinner. Maryanne ended up dropping out of school at grade three to nurse her mother through her sickness and over the course of several traumatic months, watched her mother grow thinner and weaker until eventually she succumbed to death's grip. During those turbulent months the family also found out that the youngest daughter, just five years old, was HIV positive too. Maryanne took on sole responsibility for the care of her sick family members; finding food, cooking, cleaning and looking after her younger siblings. She told me that her two younger brothers had never attended school and instead spent long days fishing to supplement the family income.

Over the course of several years, we journeyed alongside Maryanne and her younger siblings, first through the death of their mother, then the youngest girl. Maryanne found out later that her absent father had been killed in an accident. Aunty Lin took a special interest and began visiting and encouraging them almost every week, helping fix up their tiny home and mend their broken hearts.

Maryanne and her siblings became one of the first teenager-headed households in Project HALO because they had inherited their home and were keen to stay there, amongst the strong support network of their Cham community.

In Cambodia, the incidence of older orphans caring for their younger siblings is much lower than in Africa where the AIDS epidemic is being experienced on a larger scale and extended family networks have been worse hit. However, there is still a significant number of households like Maryanne's in Cambodia and I soon came to see that these households should be counted as teenager-headed long before the parents die, because of the significant caregiver role a teenager may take on when the parent becomes incapacitated due to AIDS.

Clearly these teenager-headed families were extremely vulnerable to exploitation, psychological trauma and stress, poverty, lack of opportunities to attend school and a range of other difficulties. I felt it was up to us to make their lives as trouble-free and safe as possible under the difficult circumstances.

Surprisingly perhaps, living as a teenager-headed household was the preferred option for some families, especially if they had inherited a piece of land and a house from their parents and lived in close proximity to extended family who would visit regularly and provide them with material support. For example, Maryanne's aunt next door began to feed them and they were surrounded by a tight network of relatives and friends.

Despite the challenges, Maryanne and other teenager-headed families like hers demonstrated an incredible resilience and resourcefulness in the face of extreme difficulty. The younger boys agreed to attend school if we could cover their school fees and for a time they received emergency rice supplies on a monthly basis from Project HALO. But soon, with a small business loan and some budgeting advice, Maryanne was able to earn a small living selling fish and they no longer needed this financial help. After a while, whenever we came around, the neighbours would comment quite cheerfully, 'Here come the Jesus people!' By God's grace we were planting seeds and earning some kudos for the kingdom in the midst of that Muslim community.

Across the road from Maryanne and her siblings lived another Muslim family devastated by the AIDS virus. Matt was just thirteen years old when he was orphaned but he was blessed to have a loving aunty and grandmother to take over his parents' role. Matt began to attend school with some support from Project HALO and enjoyed the opportunity to learn both the Cambodian language and the Cham language of his people.

One day, Matt was referred to our medical clinic complaining of dizziness and sore legs. A few questions, a quick inspection and we realized he was malnourished. It was not that the family was particularly lacking in food or money, but they didn't realize the importance of getting enough of the right types of food to eat, taking into account their Muslim diet restrictions. With some input from our nutrition specialist, hefty Mrs Neang, Matt made a full recovery and was able to return to school.

From time to time we held fun outings for the orphans and Matt and Maryanne and their siblings were always invited along. Because we had built up a good reputation with the Cham community they were allowed to attend, though they were careful not to eat our non-halal food. We were beginning to see the hand of God in that community, slowly but surely planting the seeds of his kingdom.

Boo, a nominal Buddhist, was another who recognized the work of God in his life. We first got to know him when one of his neighbours, a Servants volunteer, noticed that he had lost a lot of weight. She convinced Boo to visit the Servants AIDS homecare team who counselled him and sent him for testing. Unfortunately for Boo, his test came back HIV positive. Even worse, he had also passed the disease on to his wife. The weight dropped off and Boo grew increasingly emaciated and gaunt. Our homecare volunteers and staff visited him regularly to bring medicine and encouragement, and they also invited along a member of the local church to pray for Boo a number of times.

Then another shocking blow struck the family: in one terrible night they lost their tiny home and all their possessions in a raging fire that burnt down their slum. On top of this, Boo's oldest son, Lane, was learning welding, but he had to leave his course in order to work and pay back a family debt. One day, I was visiting Boo and his wife and they told me about their troubles and Lane's disappointment. 'Would you like me to pray that Jesus will help you?' I offered. They readily agreed and we prayed together. When I opened my eyes I saw that they were both moved to tears. Within two weeks, there was a breakthrough and Lane was able to return to his course. At this stage Boo's heart was softening towards God and he was making small steps in the right direction. After months of camping out in someone's flooded shed, Project HALO was able to secure a small piece of land for them to live on rent free. Lane worked alongside our Christian builder to put up a small but sturdy house.

One day, one of our volunteers sat down with Boo and pieced together the myriad of ways God had been working in his life, through prayer, practical help and little encouragements. He explained about the problem of sin and our need to receive God's forgiveness. Boo broke down in tears and declared that he wanted to be a follower of Jesus. Just weeks later, he went to be with his Lord.

The Big Brothers and Sisters

Dee and her problem kids gave us the mental shove we needed to take Project HALO to the next level. She was squatting at the local pagoda at the time, having been flooded out of her home in a nearby slum. Under one large sheet of blue plastic tarpaulin lived several extended family members and Dee with her five kids, a scruffy bunch of characters who were dispatched out onto the streets each day to collect cans and bottles which would be recycled for cash to supplement the family income. None were attending school. Dee herself was too sick to work, having contracted HIV from her late husband.

Wandering the streets looking for rubbish each day, Boon and Barn, Dee's two oldest boys, joined up for protection with other kids in the same position and a gang was formed. Oftentimes these street gangs would progress to petty theft and glue-sniffing. Both Boon and Barn were on the edges of this kind of activity and were frequently getting themselves into trouble.

One of the things that concerned me deeply about Boon and Barn was the complete lack of good role models in their lives. I realized that by the time they were orphaned, they would be firmly entrenched in a criminal lifestyle that would take them nowhere except prison.

They desperately needed someone older, wiser, someone understanding, to get alongside and encourage them in the right direction. At the same time I realized that our vision to see Cambodian communities, led by the church, caring for their own orphans was only partially being fulfilled. Certainly children were being cared for within their own communities, but our own workers and volunteers were sometimes the only representatives of the church having any input. I longed to see the church more sacrificially involved, on a wider scale.

I no longer recall exactly when or how the idea came to me, but I do remember how it struck me as an idea so simple and yet so powerful that I was certain it was a gift from God for Boon and Barn and others like them. The idea was to mobilize Christian young people to take on one orphan each as their 'little brother' or 'little sister', to visit and encourage the kids, discipling them over time and simply being good role models.

I went to share my burden with a very close friend and confidant, Pyneath, a young Cambodian man of great wisdom and insight. He was already the head of Young Life Cambodia, an organization reaching out to high school youth, and I believed that he would one day be one of the foremost Christian leaders in Cambodia. Pyneath had a cadre of high quality young Christians that he had personally discipled and I asked him to put the word out that we were looking for Big Brothers and Sisters for the orphans. Pyneath, from a poor background himself, was genuinely moved by the idea and before long he had rustled up a group of ten young Christians aged mostly around twenty, who were willing to become Big Brothers and Big Sisters. He called me up to come around and share the vision.

That first meeting, we just sat around on the floor in one of the rooms at Young Life and I shared about God's passionate and lavish love for orphans. Around the room, they sat transfixed, eyes shining, excited by the call to put their faith into practice for such an important cause. They had no idea what they were in for.

I confess to choosing my toughest and neediest kids to match up with them, including Boon and Barn and their younger sister, praying fervently that it would make a difference in these kids' lives.

It was a steep learning curve and there were things we did then that I would do differently now. One problem was that we didn't give that first bunch much training and two dropped out within a few weeks. After that, we kept making changes to the program to make it better, including adding a more comprehensive training and screening process. Pyneath and I handpicked the two guys we thought would be most likely to make progress with Boon and Barn, and in hindsight God's hand of grace was in the whole thing as well.

I was surprised to find that for many of these first Big Brothers and Sisters, it was a rude shock to be taken into a slum. Most were from relatively middle-class backgrounds and they were afraid of having their nice motorbikes stolen. But they valiantly made an effort and it is a testimony to their faithfulness that all, except the first two who quickly fell away, still continue to minister as volunteer Big Brothers and Sisters several years down the track. Quite a few of them have gone on to start their own groups of Big Brothers and Sisters in their own churches.

Boon and Barn's Big Brothers began visiting them at the pagoda. They sat and chatted with the boys for hours and took them riding around on their motorbikes all over town. As a group we all would go out on monthly outings to places like the zoo, the waterfront or the Palace, places Boon and Barn had never had the opportunity to go to. Project HALO began paying for Boon and Barn's school fees so they could return to school and their Big

Brothers really encouraged them to go by looking through their school books regularly and asking how the studies were going. But it wasn't easy. Boon and Barn were constantly dropping out of school to hang with their street friends and make some extra money recycling. Barn's Big Brother, Bisit, would often share with me his concerns about Barn's latest behaviour.

One day, Dee became pregnant again. Realising she could hardly afford to feed the kids she had, let alone another, she decided to sell the baby. Aware of many unscrupulous baby vendors and some of the horrible situations these children could end up in, we counselled her and she agreed that with a small amount of support she would try to make a go of it. We made sure she had the appropriate antiretroviral drugs at birth to avoid passing the HIV virus to her newborn baby girl: a $20-dollar medicine that could ensure the protection of a newborn child.[58] When the latest baby was born, the Big Brothers and Sisters were all around and they helped Dee choose a name from the Bible – Sarah, which means princess.

The lucky orphans chosen to participate thrived under the attention of their Big Brothers or Sisters. We matched up Sally's two grandchildren, Savouen and Layak with a Big Brother and a Big Sister each as well. Both responded immediately. Savouen in particular, at the time, was an angst-ridden adolescent, given to monosyllabic grunts. But his Big Brother La was a gentle giant with a winning grin. Savouen couldn't help but warm up under that smile.

When Sally's house burned down in a terrible fire one night, Big Brother La went to his own church and told them what had happened. He passed around the hat and raised enough money to buy them a new bed and a big sack of rice. I was impressed. Big Brother La had compassion, initiative and warmth but most importantly Savouen was making good progress under his discipleship.

As the workload was increasing steadily with growing numbers of orphans, I had been praying for God to provide a male for the Project HALO team who could complement Aunty Lin's motherly role. Thirty-year-old Big Brother La seemed the perfect choice. He had already proven himself with Savouen and I was keen to let other boys in the program benefit from the warmth and solidity of this good-hearted young man. And so, I offered Big Brother La a full-time job ministering to the now several hundred orphans in Project HALO alongside Aunty Lin. Big Brother La came on board and our full-time team grew to three. Meanwhile, the Big Brother and Sister groups also grew through word of mouth to several other churches.

Discipling Orphans

I wish I had found fourteen-year-old Arom at least a year earlier. Arom had lost his mother to AIDS and couldn't afford to continue paying rent on his tiny family home, so he hung around the only place he knew, his village. Relying on the mercy of neighbours and his wits to survive, Arom spent a year living off scraps and handouts, lacking even the basics of sufficient food, clothing and a safe place to sleep, before we found him. Arom told me later that during his homeless year, he often crept under the wooden homes in his community to sleep at night. He confided that the worst thing about this sleeping arrangement was that sometimes he would catch a deluge of urine that came through the bamboo slat floors.

Shelter is one of the most basic needs of a human being and Aunty Lin and I did a lot of work to ensure that the kids had a decent place to live. I tried not to impose Western standards on people who had grown up in the slums, nor to push our Western idea of 'basic needs' on those who had only known a simple lifestyle. We sought merely to ensure that the leaky roofs were patched up and the four walls and front door were not falling off.

One of the challenges we faced was making sure no one stole the orphans' land from under them as soon as the parents passed away. We tried to get parents to sign

over their land title and house title into the children's
names before it was too late, but most were reluctant to
deal with this rather concrete reminder of their immi-
nent death. And so we decided that this was one area
where gentle coercion would be appropriate. Whenever
anyone needed a broken roof patched or a ruined wall
fixed up, we would first help them go down to the village chief and put their land title into the kids' names –
only then we would make the arrangements for the
repair.

Sixteen-year-old Mayana's land was an extremely
frustrating case that forced us to put more energy into
this advocacy issue. Orphaned children, already vulnerable to exploitation, who inherited property from their
parents, were much more likely to retain that property if
they were present to occupy and protect it.[59] Nevertheless, there were those who would stop at nothing to rip
off an orphan if they thought they could get away with
it. That's where we came in.

Since the death of her parents, Mayana had been caring for her four younger sisters with the help of an aunt
and grandparents who lived nearby. Mayana and her
sisters were all still in school and Mayana hoped to
become a pharmacist one day like her aunt. They were
fortunate enough to have inherited an old wooden home
on stilts from their parents.

One day, we received an urgent message that some
relatives of the girls were attempting to sell the land and
house from underneath them. Aunty Lin and I took the
girls to lay a complaint at the district commune office. To
our relief, the commune leader put a bar on selling the
land until Mayana reached eighteen and could legally
retain ownership. Though the case was temporarily
solved I must admit that I retained a lot of anger
towards Mayana's dodgy relatives, wondering what

kind of person could be so greedy as to exploit orphans, and their own flesh and blood no less.

As a result of this kind of situation, we would eventually develop a system for helping parents write a last will and testament, which clearly outlined inheritance and property issues as well as their desires for the future care of the children.

Apart from shelter and property inheritance, a number of other practical matters needed to be dealt with to ensure that the kids had rice in their bowls each night and clothes on their backs. For the poorest of the poor in Cambodia, day to day life is a roller-coaster of uncertainty. They typically have multiple sources of income and on a good day they will make enough to feed the family. Other days they go hungry or are forced to take out expensive loans to pay for emergencies, particularly medical problems. These high interest loans from local lenders could multiply exponentially and quickly spiral out of control. Time and time again families lost their homes and their land over what started as a couple of hundred dollars loan.

I trained the Project HALO team to provide grass roots budgeting advice to the adults and the children and in particular to teach them how to put aside a tiny amount each day for emergencies. We provided the families with their own 'piggy banks' – a small metal box complete with padlock and key to be kept at their homes. We monitored their level of savings each month, providing encouragement and advice. Occasionally we made small business loans at no interest to help families begin earning an income. We worked closely with each family to plan for the time when they would be able to stand on their own two feet.

One of the first beneficiaries of this new service was a seventy-one-year-old grandmother, Ngaa, who had resigned herself to becoming a mother for the second time when her daughter died of AIDS leaving two vulnerable and scared little girls, Gung and Gia. Every day, Ngaa sat selling her wares from the front window of her thatch home, keeping watch over her two granddaughters who played with the neighbours and came and went happily from the local school.

Ngaa wasn't particularly keen to continue allowing Gung to pursue an education. Ngaa felt that Gung, at thirteen, had had enough schooling for a girl and it was time for her to go to work peeling garlic at a nearby factory. Besides, the profit from her tiny shop was barely enough to cover food and other expenses, let alone school fees. Sitting down with Ngaa one day, we worked out her income and her expenditure. To my surprise, we discovered that she was locked into a cycle of monthly credit with exorbitant interest payments to the local loan shark in order to pay for her stock each month.

The system was very common amongst the entrepreneurial poor and worked like this. At the start of every month, Ngaa would borrow $20 to buy the month's stock. Each day throughout the month, she would pay the loan shark $1, a total of $30 a month on average. She was paying $10 interest a month on a $20 loan!

We agreed on a small interest-free loan of $20 that would allow her to avoid taking her stock on credit the next month. She set aside $1 a day as usual, but instead of paying the loan shark, she put it into her new 'piggy bank' and repaid us our $20 at the end of the month, leaving her with $10, half the money she needed to buy another month worth of stock. One more interest-free loan of $10 the following month brought her to the place where she could pay us back completely and thereafter she was able to save $10 extra every month for expenses like the girls' schooling and medical emergencies.

The road to financial security for the poor is a mine-field. People like Ngaa were understandably extremely 'risk-averse' and nervous about diverting money away from their daily needs and the routines they were used to, even when those routines were a huge rip-off. It took a lot of explaining and convincing before Ngaa was willing to give our system a go. I believed the onus was on us to demonstrate the value of saving for emergencies and assist them to do so.

Another family we introduced the 'piggy bank' to was a family of teenage orphans headed by nineteen-year-old Arit. The teens had lost both their parents to AIDS within the space of a month. Still, Arit was an optimistic, upbeat young guy who had taken on a lot of responsibility. Every evening, Arit returned home from his job as a coal porter covered in black dust and aching from the hard physical work of riding his bicycle up and down with a heavy trailer behind. He complained of sometimes feeling dizzy while riding, which we attributed to lack of food since he confessed he was missing meals.

We offered Arit some basic tips about setting aside a little of his income each day, helping him project to see how much he would save in one month, ten months, or a couple of years down the track. Arit saw that with diligence, he would be able to afford a motorcycle, which would help with his work.

Arit's excitement about the new piggy bank saving scheme caught on amongst his younger siblings and his two youngest brothers went out and bought themselves a little box too. Before long, all four teenagers were saving and I followed Arit's progress towards the motorbike with interest.

One day, I asked how the saving was going and Arit's sixteen-year-old sister Sokun said, 'Great!' and thrust out her hand, proudly showing off a new 24-carat gold ring.

I tried not to show my disappointment. 'But you were doing so well, you were well on your way to having enough money for a motorbike. Why did you blow it on a ring?'

Sokun patiently gave me a lesson in Cambodian saving methods. 'Look at our home.' She gestured at the thatch walls of their tiny room. 'It's not safe to leave a box with money in here for too long, even a metal box with a padlock. Someone will steal it.' She waved the ring in my face again, giggling. 'So we turn the money into something portable, something that can be exchanged for cash any time we need it.'

A big grin spread over my face, and I nodded. 'You are one smart little lady!'

My urban poor friends like Arit and Sokun did not trust the banks and they introduced me to another common financial practice known in Cambodia as *Tong Teng* – a grassroots savings and loans scheme which brings people together in groups to save and lend to each other. We encouraged these local solutions on a purely pragmatic basis, because they seemed to work. Drawing on the *Tong Teng* concept, another Servants team mate had set up a micro-credit program where poor women got themselves together in groups to take out small business loans. Since the group paid back the loan together, there was peer pressure on each woman to make sure she paid her share. At its peak, the micro credit project was reaching over a thousand women.

Despite the many small-scale successes, we were constantly being hampered by a lack of government support, even opposition at times. One of the largest slums in Cambodia, on the opposite riverbank from our place at the End of the Road, was being targeted for eviction by the city authorities. One day, the local newspaper showed an artist's rendition of the dreams the city mayor had for turning Phnom Penh into a tourist Mecca. The drawing showed Western-looking people strolling happily along a boardwalk at the river's edge. There were no slums in sight of course, and for obvious reasons the drawing did not include the beggars or poor people who normally frequented these places. The drawing was an ominous foreshadowing of what was to come.

One night, after months of fruitless negotiation with the community who refused to budge, the government took matters into their own hands and a single fiery flare shot from a passing boat right into the flammable mass of thatch huts jammed at the river's edge. At least a thousand families lost their homes and their hard-earned possessions in the resulting fire, which had people scrambling for their lives.

In the morning, having just found out about the blaze, I rushed over to the still-smouldering community, looking for a family of three kids I had spent time with just the day before. Thirteen-year-old Sonti and her two younger brothers had recently nursed both parents to their deaths by AIDS. With their mother dead barely a few weeks, they were grieving, but proud of the new home we had built them with the help of neighbours and relatives. It was the first night they were able to sleep in the tiny house.

I caught sight of Sonti squatting on the scorched earth, the very spot where her new home should have been standing. She buried her face in her hands and shook her head. 'Everything's gone.' I knew that 'everything' included her most precious possession: the only photo of her dead mother. She had already known more tragedy than I had met in my whole lifetime.

'Get your brothers and come with me. You can stay at my house!' I choked with emotion.

Sonti shook her head. 'If we leave, who's to say we ever lived here? We have to stay put so we can be sure of getting any help that comes!'

I knew she was in for a punishing day under the blazing sun with no shelter and then a cold night without blankets. But she was not to be persuaded, so I promised to see what I could do and hurried off to the Servants office.

An emergency planning meeting was already underway by the time I got there. Someone was put in charge of immediately contacting the local authorities to obtain permission to distribute emergency supplies, and we requested a list of names of those registered as living in the slum. But we had not bargained on total opposition from the government.

We were informed that we were not allowed to distribute so much as one grain of rice, since this would constitute encouraging these people to stay on the land. We were dumbstruck. To attempt an emergency distribution without the permission and help of the local authorities was not only illegal and dangerous – it was also extremely difficult because we would not have access to their lists of residents. We called a prayer and planning meeting of local churches and Christian groups and explained the situation. We emailed prayer groups back home and asked them to begin interceding for us.

From the office, I went to visit Pyneath, my friend at Young Life and asked if he could round up some volunteers. Pyneath and his students were keen to be involved even though they knew it would mean danger for themselves.

The next day, like undercover agents, our teams of Christian volunteers worked their way painstakingly through the burned slum, distributing tickets to 1,000 desperate and destitute families plot by plot. Near the end, word began to spread amongst the fire victims that tickets were being given out for an emergency distribution. Mothers, frantically worried for their hungry children, begged for tickets. Others, distressed and some hysterical, pleaded and jostled for tickets and things began to get out of hand. One of our helpers, a petite middle-class Cambodian girl, found herself swept up in a tide of desperate people grabbing and crying. She finally escaped shaken and scratched but otherwise unhurt.

The emergency supplies had to be located out of the sight of the local authorities who had denied permission for the distribution, so we used a patch of land where we normally held clinics, about a mile away from that slum. Streams of people made their way from the scorched riverbank to the distribution site, clutching their tickets.

Long lines formed and the distribution began, peacefully at first. But just hours into the operation, bad news began to filter back to us. Reports were coming in that the local authorities had found out about our act of civil disobedience. Cunningly, rather than breaking up our distribution party, they had positioned armed soldiers around the corner to confiscate the supplies from people returning to the slum. This way, they could both stop the desperate people from getting the emergency supplies and enjoy the proceeds themselves.

Then Rick, a missionary friend of ours, called to see if everything was all right. In frustration, we explained what was going on and he decided to come down to the riverside to see if there was anything he could do to help. The tide was about to turn.

Kristin was already deep in negotiation with the soldiers when Rick arrived on the scene dressed up in a suit and tie because he was on his way to church. The soldiers looked at him incredulously, then their unease turned to alarm as a murmur began to spread through the group of troopers. Somehow they had got the idea that our friend Rick was the American Ambassador. And Kristin was doing nothing to dissuade them from their error! The soldiers looked at each other in panic and then someone barked out an order. Promptly, they began unloading the supplies and drove away. We were free to continue with no further harassment. We finished the distribution without further problems and a few days later the government had a change of heart and asked us to help with further emergency aid.

But short-term relief only goes so far. Sonti and her brothers, their immediate needs temporarily alleviated by some rice, a mosquito net, a plastic tarpaulin and some other bits and pieces, were nevertheless still homeless.

Word came down that the government was planning to implement its original eviction plans, which meant trucking everyone to a large relocation site twenty miles outside the city. This time the community was in no position to negotiate. Spirits broken, they resigned themselves to the move and lined up en masse under the scorching sun to register for their new plot.

The relocation took place before the site had been prepared and so Sonti and her brothers found themselves along with about five thousand other refugees in the middle of nowhere: no running water, no electricity, no sewage system, no schools, markets or any other support structures in place to deal with the mass of humanity under blue plastic.

Because they had previously been in a Christian orphanage, Sonti and her brothers were highly suspicious of Christians. We made the trek almost daily at first, following up with Sonti and the several other Project HALO and AIDS homecare families that had been relocated, but Sonti remained surly and uncooperative. She wanted to wait for the allocation of their plot before she would consider going back to the city. Her uncle convinced me that he would keep an eye on them so I reluctantly agreed to let the situation continue a while longer, thinking that the government would allocate the plots at any moment. Days stretched into weeks and weeks blurred into months. Eventually they were given a tiny corner of dirt, with nothing on it. A school had been set up and conditions were improving, but Sonti and her brothers were still struggling and finally we came to the point where we felt it was absolutely essential to relocate them back to Phnom Penh. They took some convincing, but finally, with the erection of a little fence around their new plot and the promise that they could come back to keep an eye on it anytime they liked, they capitulated and we loaded up the few pots and pans and assorted clothing they had to shift them back to the city.

Vee's neighbour, a lady who had become a Christian through the fledgling fellowship that had been sparked there, agreed to take them into her household and provide some guidance. So Sonti and her brothers quietly unpacked the few things they had and settled into their new home, the third in six months.

As they got to know the new place and community they were drawn into the vibrant church birthed through the original group of seekers. Slowly, I saw them open up and change. Sonti became cheerful again and her brothers became avid students of the Bible, often copying out passages that interested them in the evenings and diligent in their daily prayers. The transformation was really quite remarkable. Project HALO was still providing rice, and other basic necessities, but the Christian community in that place gathered around them and provided the emotional and spiritual support, the sense of family they were desperately lacking.

Nay had been unable to return to the brothel clinic after the birth of Jayden but she was keen to become involved again in some kind of child-friendly ministry. Gathering together Sonti and a small group of other teenage girls from Project HALO, she began a daily discipleship and income generation program. Each morning Nay and her girls, with Jayden tagging along as well, met to make greeting cards and other crafts for sale. As they worked, they talked incessantly and encouraged one another. Before long, Nay and the girls had developed some good designs and Nay sold them to tourist shops around the city and to visitors, some who would even take them back to sell in the West. A steady little income was helping Sonti and her friends contribute to the needs of their families and siblings.

Discipleship was becoming a major thrust of Project HALO, especially for the teenagers who were facing all the extra baggage and complications of learning what it means to become an adult. Once again I turned for help to my Young Life friend.

'Pyneath,' I pointed out over coffee one day, 'Young Life in America concentrates on high schools and that gives them contact with most teenagers in the States. But if you only target high schools here in Cambodia, you are missing a huge proportion of the teenagers. You are effectively ignoring the poor, all those teenagers who can't afford an education, or have been delayed at school because they need to help out at home with sick parents.'

Pyneath nodded slowly, knowing he was about to hear another one of my hare-brained schemes that would no doubt involve him, and I continued, 'Why don't we partner together to set up a training and discipleship centre that specifically targets poor and orphaned teenagers? I've got 200 teenagers affected by AIDS in the program who are crying out for discipleship, mentoring and some vocational training. They all live around this area.' I waved my arm around at the slums surrounding the café.

Pyneath agreed to give it a go and before long we had rented a small building just twenty metres from where we sat that day, for the princely sum of $150 a month. Nay's card-makers were the first regular participants, and before long we were running English and computer classes as well.

Pyneath sent Sopee, one of his best staff, over to the centre to get things off the ground. Sopee was a cuddly young guy with a passion for discipleship. Before long he was joined by Guntee, a slightly serious bespectacled young woman, also on fire for God.

Sopee and Guntee began to visit all the teenagers in Project HALO at their homes, getting to know them and inviting them to participate in the various activities happening at the centre. Our vision was to create a sort of 'all hours' drop-in centre, a place where these kids could feel welcome and safe, a safe haven.

Some of our teenagers were already in vocational training at other places. A few cycled across town to study electronics or hairdressing at a well-known centre run by a secular organization.

Our Young Life/Project HALO training centre was becoming more popular. A core group of about twenty teenagers were especially committed to coming. Several months before, I had taken them to see a data entry company with a mission to assist the community. They particularly tried to hire disabled people and older orphans.

So we gathered a bunch of teenagers and took them over there to inspire them. These kids formed the core of people at the training centre in those early days.

But what really encouraged me was to see the support they offered each other. Sopee and Guntee were discipling these teenagers and over time, most of them became strong Christians. All of them faced similar difficulties because their parents were HIV positive or had already died of AIDS. Every now and then, one of their parents would die. It was a devastating time for any teenager to go through, but these kids benefited from the support group they had around them at the training centre. They developed a routine. Whenever one of their parents died, they would send word to their friends who would hold a prayer meeting to pray for their bereaved friend and then go all together to the funeral in a show of solidarity. There's no way we could have manipulated such a wonderful Spirit-led response; it was just another aspect of God's grace in those kids' lives.

As Sopee and Guntee discipled more kids and continued their regular visits to their homes, they began to invite the older teens who were becoming stronger in the faith to accompany them. And so, we began to catch a glimpse of what it might look like to come full circle. Orphans who had benefited from the love and support of others were now willing to become wounded healers and extend this love and support to others.[60] It was a very encouraging development.

There was one other development I didn't notice at first though; Big Brother La had taken quite a shine to Guntee.

Spreading the Word

People inside and outside Cambodia were beginning to sit up and take notice of what was going on in Project HALO. UNICEF contacted me saying they wanted to come see what we were doing and eventually they ended up writing it all up as a case study in best practice. Invitations came from various secular and Christian groups to speak and share the Project HALO story.

On occasion, I accepted these opportunities to tell our story because I felt frustrated that in Asia, unlike Africa, community-based care for orphans was largely unknown, misunderstood or ignored. Project HALO was the first community-based orphan care project ever established in Cambodia and I was struggling to find anyone doing anything similar in any of our neighbouring countries. The orphanage or 'children's home' model was still alive and spreading.

On one occasion I was invited to Malaysia to speak to a mixed group of leaders of children's ministry, including several who had established orphanages. Others were just beginning to consider how they might become more involved in orphan ministry. Several crossed arms told me I had a tough crowd before I even began. So, to break the ice we went around introducing ourselves and I showed a short video on our ministry. Then I put up my first PowerPoint slide.

> **Community-based care for orphans
> means care for children by those who
> are not the biological parents but are
> able to provide individual care and
> nurture in the context of a family and
> community. Most community-based
> care programs have a strong
> 'prevention' component because they
> are seeking to strengthen community
> coping capacities in order to avoid the
> institutionalization of the child.**

'Look,' I smiled at the circle of inscrutable faces, 'I'm sure you all agree that children need more than just good physical care? Children need more than just food, clothing and shelter.' Heads nodded. 'I would suggest that they also need the nurture, love, individual attention, identity and social connections that families and communities can provide. In fact, I want to tell you about a guy named John Bowlby and his fascinating discoveries about the need for a mother substitute . . .' And I went on to share the basic outline of attachment theory.

Looking around the room, about half were Westerners and half were Asians. 'Sometimes we can be fooled into thinking that a child who has lost their parents has lost everything and everyone important. But in the non-Western world there is a much greater importance placed on extended family, even distant relatives, and the surrounding community. Neighbours know each other intimately and privacy is largely non-existent.' An Indian lady and several of the other Asians were nodding in agreement, so I made my point. 'Children who are able to stay in their own communities benefit from access to these support networks throughout the rest of their lives. Community-based care allows these kids to stay within the network of people who have ties to the biological parents: uncles who grew up working the fields with Dad, aunts who gossiped over a soup pot with Mum, neighbours who knew Mum and Dad since they were young and who would have tales to share for years to come. These children have lost their parents, why take them away from everyone else they know and love?'

I could see that the ice was beginning to thaw as curiosity took over. The Indian woman adjusted her sari and I clicked on to the next PowerPoint slide.

> **Community-based care allows children to stay within the network of people that have loved and nurtured them throughout their lives. The orphaned child who grows up in a family environment close to their original community will be able to remain connected with their family and heritage and this gives a sense of rootedness and stability that is vital in the midst of turmoil and change brought on by bereavement.**

'The longer children stay in orphanages, children's homes or other forms of residential care, the more likely they are to be detached from community life,' I explained. 'A good knowledge of our family origin is very important in the development and preservation of a personal identity.[61] Children in community-based care will be more likely to hear and learn stories about their family and forebears. These stories and other pieces of information will be built up over time as the child interacts with neighbours and extended family and play an essential role in helping the child to feel that they are part of a network of people with a unique history. You simply cannot replicate that in an orphanage. Children raised in orphanages and children's homes, separated from their communities, grow into adulthood and have difficulty reintegrating into society.' I paused. 'Any questions so far?'

An American woman indicated with a slight wave that she had a question. 'But can relatives really help these orphans? I mean, they are often so destitute themselves, with their own kiddies too. Surely it would be better to put the orphans in a loving, Christian, children's home?'

'Well, in my experience working with hundreds of families, relatives generally feel a greater sense of duty and responsibility than unrelated people to provide good quality care and nurturing to the orphans. But the problem is they often don't believe in their own ability or capacity to help. They see the bright shiny orphanage down the road and assume the orphans will be better off there. But, who would be more likely to be committed to those children long term, even AFTER they have grown up and still need the family connections and sense of heritage that extended family provide?' I asked the American woman.

'Of course,' I conceded, 'sometimes the extended family is non-existent or unable to provide for orphans.' This new direction brought a vigorous nodding of heads so I went on to acknowledge that some children do slip through the cracks and end up in a variety of vulnerable situations. 'We all know of children living and working on the streets, working for other people in unpaid domestic or agricultural settings, or living by themselves with their brothers and sisters in child-headed households.'

'Yeah, what about those children?' interjected the American woman on behalf of a few others who were now leaning forward in their seats.

'These children need extra special attention and support from people like us in order to enable them to develop and thrive,' I expounded. 'Foster parents especially, but also well-supported teenager-headed households in certain circumstances, and other creative solutions may form the basis of a community-based solution for these children who for one reason or another are unable to stay with extended family. But, and it's a very big BUT, experience shows that outsiders wildly overestimate the numbers of children that are unable to be cared for by extended family, if only they were given a little support. Research shows that these children make up only around two to three per cent of the total number of orphans, even in countries all over Africa where the prevalence of HIV is very high.[62] Here in Asia, the AIDS epidemic is nowhere near affecting the proportions in Africa, so extended family networks are still mostly intact.'

Then I shared a confession, 'When we started Project HALO we spent a lot of time recruiting foster families from local churches. We trained them, we interviewed them, we screened them. And at the end of the day, when we had eliminated all those who were unsuitable for one reason or another, we still had a good bunch of at least forty foster families who were just about banging down our door to take in orphans as their own. I confess that we still have not used those foster families, despite helping hundreds and hundreds of destitute and orphaned children, for one simple but important reason. We completely underestimated the strength and willingness of the extended family. We do not have too few foster parents; we have too many children needlessly taken from their own homes! Grandmas who were asking us where the local orphanage is so they could drop off their grandchildren, came to realize they could cope with a little assistance. Aunts and uncles who despaired of being able to take in another four children, are on their feet and thriving. To this day, those foster families we recruited think we were just messing them around, playing games, because we still haven't done an informal adoption. We still have them on our books, but I'm pretty sure we will never need them. Grandma and Grandpa, Aunty and Uncle are out there and they are scared but willing to try. Maybe, doubting their own abilities, and recognizing that they are too poor to cope, they will decide that the child is better off in an orphanage. But with a little bit of support, they will make better caregivers for their orphaned relatives than the most highly trained, loving staff member ever will because they love those kids as their own flesh and blood. It's not a job to them, it's not a role they will tearfully kiss goodbye to when the child turns eighteen. It's a lifelong relationship.'

I looked around the room, scanning each face for a sign that they were with me. I knew these leaders would have influence over thousands of children's lives. I hoped they were becoming as convinced as I was that a loving, stable, one-on-one parental-type relationship is as critical to the young child's survival and health as is food and health care.[63] For orphans this means a nurturing, long-term 'mother substitute', especially in Asia where extended family and the community are the principal social safety nets. I wanted the group to really see that not having such connections greatly increases long-term vulnerability.

I decided to move on from the psychosocial issues to discuss economic and developmental reasons why I had come to prefer the community-based approach. Though I didn't say it, it seemed a great shame to me that Christian organizations, secular groups, even governments were prepared to spend serious money every week on orphanage care for children but would never think to give a couple of bucks to a widow, an unmarried mother, or a grandmother to help her care for the kids at home.

John Bowlby, architect of attachment theory, put the case even more forcefully when he said, 'Nothing is more characteristic of the shameful attitudes towards this problem than the willingness to spend large sums of money looking after children away from their homes, in stark contrast with a haggling stinginess in giving aid to the home itself.'[64]

'Of course, it's not all about money,' I continued. 'The bean counters will never convince me that cost-effectiveness is more important than the best quality care for the children. And I would rather spend a million dollars on looking after a child well than save a million by leaving a child neglected. But the wise stewardship of the resources God has given us, demands that we take into account the vast and overwhelming weight of the research that has been carried out in this field and put our dollars where they will be most effective.'

I passed around some handouts explaining, 'Community-based care for orphans is a vastly more cost-effective approach to orphan care because the emphasis is not on providing resources from outside, but on identifying the existing resources in a community and building on those. World Bank research has found that orphanage care is six times more expensive than foster care, while comparisons elsewhere show the ratio of operating costs for orphanage care to be anything up to a hundred times more expensive.'[65] I waved the documents about.

A few people whistled through their teeth at the figures. Other shook their heads slowly.

'This is a major tenet of the Servants approach to mission. Jesus didn't come to earth hurling thunderbolts and calling up his armies of angels. Instead he came to us vulnerable and lowly, not expecting to be served but to serve others. And so, in Servants we do not come initially as powerful bearers of outside resources, expertise and cash. But rather we come as learners intent on helping urban poor communities discover and identify the resources that God has already blessed them with. The best community-based care programs rely more on the existing resources in a community than on what is available from outside the community, so there is less dependency on outside funding and a greater sense of community ownership. In developing countries where the political situation is fluid, no foreign missionary, no matter how committed, can guarantee their long-term presence or access to resources, so sustainability must be built into any ministry from the very beginning. It is important to help communities recognize and mobilize their own resources, and the greatest resource of a community is its people.'[66]

The resources of the urban poor. I knew it sounded like an oxymoron. But living amongst the urban poor as an insider had helped me not to see my neighbours as suffering victims that needed me to rescue them, but instead to recognize that they are complex, resilient, blessed human beings created in God's image. The group looked a little dubious so I described the way we often challenge community folk to recognize the resources God has blessed them with.

'Here's a simple idea to help people see that God can use them,' I said. 'First we call a volunteer to come up to the front and we ask them what resources they have to offer help to an orphan. Invariably the answer is something along the lines that they have nothing, they are poor. Then we point at their feet and say "God gave you these two feet to go and visit an orphan." We lift up one of the volunteer's hands and say, "God blessed you with two hands that you can use to help fix a leaky roof, dig a vegetable garden or give a little child a hug. God blessed you with a mouth to speak up on behalf of orphans who are being exploited or to encourage an orphan who is feeling sad. You can use that God-given mouth to go to an orphan and say God loves you and so do I. And you can use your two God-given ears to sit and listen to the child as they tell you about something as mundane as school that day or something as traumatic as how they felt when they saw their mother die. Every single person sitting here today has a wealth of God-given resources that you can use to help orphans. This is not about money! This is about something much more important than cash, something that every one of us needs. It's the love and encouragement of someone who thinks we are special!"'

I looked around the room and there were smiles on many faces as they connected with the example I had given. A Filipino man who hadn't spoken up to this point clapped his hands together and declared heartily, 'I can imagine doing that! The people in the church I work at would respond to that kind of simple challenge.' Others murmured in agreement.

'Great! The whole point about community-based care is that we are building the capacity of a community to face future difficulties and thus we are inherently creating sustainability,' I continued. 'For example, we have found in Project HALO that the simple process of talking with parents and extended families about the variety of options for the future care of their orphaned children helps them to identify resources and support networks that they were previously unaware of. In almost every case, admission to orphanages was avoided by working with vulnerable families and providing a tiny amount of financial assistance, such as school fees, to parents or relatives.

'Since community-based programs are limited only by the capacity of the community rather than the availability of outside resources they are able to reach very large numbers of orphaned children with limited resources.'[67]

Someone made a slight motion with their hand to indicate that they had a question. 'Yes?' I raised my eyebrows in the direction of the questioner, an Indian man dressed in dress pants and a long-sleeved shirt, despite the heat outside.

'Well, I was just wanting to ask whether community capacity to absorb orphans could be exhausted, such as in some parts of Africa where much of the extended family networks have been wiped out by AIDS?'

I shook my head. 'Even throughout sub-Saharan Africa the extended family safety net is still by far the most effective response to economic and social crises.[68] You may be interested to know that the governments of Ethiopia, Rwanda and Uganda have recently joined the West in banning the building of any more orphanages despite their rampant AIDS epidemics. In a low prevalence country such as Cambodia and most other parts of Asia, though devastated by three decades of civil war, and with a couple of hundred thousand people living with HIV/AIDS, the capacity of the community is still much greater than that of orphanages which are constrained by buildings and staff numbers. Also, the capacity of the community can be strengthened over time by their participation in solving their own problems. This is why we emphasize the importance of a sense of community "ownership" for care of children and community involvement in the decisions, awareness raising and solutions for orphans in need of assistance. After twenty-five years of working in urban poor communities, Servants has found that the participation of the poor themselves in decision making and control of initiatives is a crucial ingredient that can make or break a project.

'There is an extremely high degree of community participation in community-based care programs because the onus is on communities to care for their own orphans. Extended families will frequently take sole responsibility for many orphans, using their own resources to provide accommodation, food, clothing, education and nurture. Neighbours and local organizations such as churches can make a tangible contribution by helping out struggling families with child-minding, food and so on. In Cambodia, a visit by community-based care program staff to a family will usually end up with the neighbours crowding in the doorway to participate in the conversation and they often end up becoming part of the solution themselves.'

The Indian man moved his head from side to side and leaned forward, resting his elbows on his knees, 'But I have heard that orphans taken in by relatives are not treated equally or may be subject to abuse by the extended family. Wouldn't it be better to take the children away from that dangerous situation and give them stability in an orphanage?'

I gently suggested that perhaps he was throwing the baby out with the bath water: 'Wherever you have more than one person under the same roof, there is a risk that one person will abuse another. This is as much of a risk for children living with their biological parents as it is for children living with relatives or in an orphanage. Let me show you what the research has indicated. Though several studies have demonstrated that orphans are disadvantaged compared to non-orphans in other families, few, if any, have demonstrated significant differences in the ways relatives treat their own biological children compared to fostered children.[69] What is clear is that when poor families take in orphans, all children in the household suffer to some extent since household spending is redistributed among a larger number of children. That is why we need community-based care programs to support these children and ensure that they are not disadvantaged or abused.'

I felt strongly that the phantom of potential abuse was often used as a smokescreen to justify the institutionalization of children. Nevertheless, I was determined to face this issue head on and ensure to the best of my ability that no child in Project HALO was ever subjected to abuse or exploitation. I shared with the group about measures we had put in place to ensure that orphans in the community were protected. We had established a Child Protection Policy and the Project HALO staff were trained to identify symptoms and deal with situations of abuse.

'Abuse or neglect that occurs in the community, particularly close-knit communities in the developing world, is much more likely to be discovered or known about than abuse that occurs in a closed residential facility. Though discovery does not necessarily lead to action, it is still an important first step in the process towards resolution. Having good policies is never going to prevent every possible case and we all know of abuse cases in orphanages and in the community. But the key is monitoring and follow-up.'

My mind ran back to one harrowing case. A woman notorious for trafficking girls for sex slavery was in the process of taking over guardianship of her two recently bereaved Project HALO nieces. Word on the street was that she planned to send them to Malaysia. We went down to talk to the girls concerned and sure enough they were naively looking forward to their upcoming trip. We called in the local village chief and explained the situation to him. He placed a great deal of pressure on the aunt to sign over her nieces to our care.

Monitoring and meticulous follow-up was an integral part of Project HALO from the start and helped to ensure that unequal treatment, abuse, or exploitation did not go unresolved. Community members themselves also participated in monitoring these households to verify that children were not being abused or exploited.[70]

In another case, we placed a little girl named Lina with a pastor and his wife who had volunteered to foster a child, since their own children were all now teenagers or married adults. Lina's mother was in the last stages of full-blown AIDS and she was desperate to see that her daughter would be well cared for in a Christian family. She claimed she had no other family.

The pastor and his wife came to meet Lina's mother and Lina for the first time, bringing a basket of fruit and assuring her that they would take good care of Lina. Later they brought back church members on a regular basis to pray and encourage her right through the final days of her life. I thought it was a wonderful situation, under the circumstances. We continued to monitor Lina's placement and she seemed to be doing well. But about six months down the track, church members sent word to us that the pastor's wife had been overzealous in her physical discipline of Lina more than once. She had crossed the line into physical abuse. I was very upset that we had failed Lina in this way and removed her immediately. Aunty Lin ended up taking Lina into her own household.

Lina's problem occurred in the early days of Project HALO and in hindsight I was not sure it was the best response. What alternatives did poor Cambodian parents have to hitting as discipline? Time out proved fairly difficult in a one-room shack. Removing privileges is impossible when the family live hand to mouth anyway and there are no luxuries such as video games or pocket money to take away. With the benefit of a few more years experience I knew it would take a great deal of creativity and wisdom to bring culturally appropriate behaviour change into this context.

As I shared our own struggles in this area, others opened up and began to share their own difficulties.

Someone asked about dealing with grief and with a sly smile I drew a bag of balloons out of my pocket. I had been waiting for this question. Handing each person a balloon I explained that in many Asian cultures grief and bad feelings are suppressed. Buddhism teaches that suffering is an illusion and anger is a sin, so we immediately came up against a cultural wall when we began to assist children to talk through their feelings of grief. But early on, I had discovered a simple little exercise that cut right through all the cultural obstacles and helped people to see the need for letting their feelings out. 'Anyone who has ever felt HAPPY blow into your balloon.' Lips pursed and puffing ensued. 'Anyone who has ever felt SAD blow into your balloon.

'Angry!' Puff. 'Hurt!' Wheeze. 'Excited!' some of the balloons were reaching their capacity. 'Frustrated?' BANG. My balloon popped and the whole room broke into laughter.

Then I looked serious. 'That balloon is like our heart. If we keep bottling up our feelings and never give them an outlet, we'll run into problems. We need to find ways to let the air out of the balloon before it explodes. And we need to find healthy ways to let out all the feelings that are getting bottled up in our heart.' The atmosphere in the room was electric with excitement at this simple idea and people began whispering and jotting down notes, heads nodding. I reached into my briefcase to pull out a sky-blue coloured book. 'That little exercise cuts through all the cultural myths and people are immediately eager to know how they can let their feelings out. We usually explain to them that crying can be healthy, talking and drawing pictures are also good. Then we show them this Memory Book we developed especially for the Asian context. We all know that a death in the family can have a devastating effect on a young life. However, we also know that with appropriate support and information, children can be helped to understand what has happened and can learn to live with their loss.' I opened the colourful book and flipped through some of the pages, pointing out simple activities to help children talk about their feelings and remember their parents.

Finally, I glanced at my watch and saw that our time was up. 'Sorry folks, that's all the time we have today. But if you have any questions I'd be happy to talk to you afterwards.'

A small crowd of people gathered around afterwards, smiling and chatting excitedly.

'Thank you so much.' The Filipino man pumped my hand. 'I've never heard that perspective before. Can I get a copy of your video to show at my church? I'm really excited about what we may be able to do in my community.'

Several others were waiting to shake my hand or ask questions and I promised to send them copies of the video, the Memory Book or other resources. At last I was left alone with my thoughts and as I packed up my papers I offered a prayer of thanks to God for each person who had sat in that room, each with a call and a passion to help orphan children. 'Lord, give us the wisdom to do right by these children,' I whispered.

A Social Movement for the Orphans

Simply through word of mouth, more and more Big Brothers and Big Sisters were volunteering from local churches to take on an orphan each. In a country where the concept of volunteerism is not widely understood, we were pioneering new inroads into the culture.

But God still had something much bigger and better in mind. He used Jean Webster, a softly-spoken motherly missionary who had pioneered Zimbabwe Orphans through Extended hands (ZOE) in Zimbabwe, to birth in me a paradigm shift in my thinking about the Big Brothers and Sisters. Through ZOE, Jean had catalyzed the Zimbabwean church to care for more than ten thousand orphans. She was intrigued by our Big Brothers and Sisters and asked me to tell her all about it. Afterwards, she challenged me, 'Craig, I believe that if you want to see the Holy Spirit spread this throughout Cambodia, you need to remove every kind of foreign obstacle, so that they can run with it themselves rather than being held back by your funding constraints.'

'But we don't provide any financial incentives at all,' I protested. 'Sure, we pay for the monthly outings but . . .' Like a flash, I could see the impediment. Jean and I bent our heads and prayed quietly together in the corner of the noisy meeting room. With tears welling in my eyes, I prayed together with Jean that Big Brothers and Sisters would spread like wildfire throughout Cambodia

and touch the lives of thousands of orphans and
Christian youth.

From that moment I knew things had to change, but I
dreaded telling the Big Brothers and Sisters that we
would stop underwriting their monthly outings, the
only tangible support we were giving. Instead, we wanted them to make even more of a sacrifice and pay for
the outings themselves. I prepared myself for a backlash
or maybe even a mass walkout. Would they all just quit
over what could seem like outright selfishness on our
part?

The meeting day arrived and biting my tongue I rose
to announce that I had something I wanted to say. The
crowd of Big Brothers and Sisters hushed and looked at
me expectantly. Hesitantly at first, I explained the vision
I felt God had given me to see Christian Big Brothers and
Sisters taking on orphans all over Cambodia, not just
Project HALO kids but vulnerable children in remote
towns and villages country-wide. Wherever there were
Christian youth, there would be Big Brothers and Sisters.
But, I whispered, there was an obstacle preventing us
pursuing that vision. By using outside money to pay for
the monthly outings, we had created a system that relied
on Western resources. It might be viable now with just a
handful of groups, but what if there were hundreds or
even thousands of groups all over the country? We had
set up a system that would be difficult to replicate on a
wider scale. Growing louder and more confident now, I
enthused, 'This needs to be Cambodian-led, Cambod-
ian-resourced and Cambodian-controlled if it is ever
going to be more than just a community development
program run by a Western mission agency.' I asked them
to pray with me, that God would anoint a Cambodian
leader to lead this movement and see it spread to every
corner of this nation.

Over the next couple of weeks I waited to see the repercussions. How many would quit? I wondered nervously. But nothing happened. A few weekends later I visited a group of Big Brothers and Sisters who had gathered their little brothers and sisters together for a game of soccer. I choked up when I saw them making several trips backwards and forwards on their motorbikes to pick up the orphans. Food was produced from somewhere and shared amongst the kids. I shook my head and whispered a silent prayer of thanks for the grace and compassion God had provided, despite my own mistakes.

I had put Big Brother La in charge of coordinating these groups, but with his own workload of visiting the now several hundred orphans in Project HALO, he had little time to put into it, beyond the weekly meeting with group leaders. We were merely reacting to the movement rather than actively pursuing and promoting the vision.

I began to pray even more fervently that God would show me who should lead the movement. Expectantly, I looked at each of the group leaders and even the various Big Brothers and Sisters in their teams. But no one seemed right. Sometimes I felt led to share the vision outside the groups of existing Big Brothers and Sisters. At one stage I was sure that I had found the right person. But once again God closed the door.

One morning, over a pot of coffee, I shared the vision with Brian Maher, who along with Uon Seila ran the youth arm of the Evangelical Fellowship of Cambodia (EFC), known as the 'Youth Commission'. As the umbrella group for virtually every church in Cambodia, they were a key stakeholder in the Big Brothers and Sisters vision, to reach out through the youth groups of the nation. Brian was intrigued and the conversation quickly shifted to a discussion of how we could do it in partnership with the EFC Youth Commission. But first he needed to talk to Seila and their Board of Advisors.

A few months later I was summoned to the Board meeting to defend the idea of launching Big Brothers and Sisters through the EFC Youth Commission. On the way, I prayed that God would give me the words to say and that, God willing, the Board would accept the proposal.

This time my audience was made up of a number of the most respected pastors and Christian leaders in Cambodia. Swallowing my nervousness, I began with an impassioned plea on behalf of the orphans of Cambodia: 'Seventy-seven thousand children in this nation have nursed their mother and their father to their death by AIDS. What is the church doing for them? How are the Christian youth you target with your programs putting their faith into practice?' I went on as a few began to nod, 'Imagine the impact we could have if every Christian youth in Cambodia took on one unchurched orphan child as their little brother or little sister. This Big Brothers and Sisters thing is so simple yet so powerful . . .'

'But why do you need to do this through the Evangelical Fellowship of Cambodia?' interrupted one pastor. 'Couldn't you just set up your own Non-Government Organization?'

Another pastor interjected, addressing the first pastor, 'If some group calling themselves Big Brothers and Sisters of Cambodia came to my church and wanted to talk to my youth, I'd be saying "Hang on! Who are you? What do you want? What right do you have to come here?" But if the EFC Youth Commission came, it would be an open door. I can see why it would be good to partner with the Youth Commission . . .'

'You're absolutely right,' I agreed. 'We need the Evangelical Fellowship of Cambodia, because Big Brothers and Sisters of Cambodia should be owned and controlled by the Cambodian church itself. Plus, the EFC Youth Commission has an open invitation into almost every Christian youth group in the land.'

A gruff-looking guy at the back raised his voice. 'Then what's in it for the Youth Commission? Aren't you just using us as a vehicle to achieve your own vision?'

'This is the vision of the Youth Commission!' I countered. 'You want to equip Christian Youth. Well, this is finally something they can do to make a contribution to the Kingdom of God in Cambodia. Rather than becoming theologically obese, by spending all their time in Bible study, with no opportunity for a practical outworking; rather than waiting till they are old enough to become pastors or church leaders, let's give them a positive role right now in the church and in their communities. What could be a better outworking of their faith than to take on a struggling child and mentor, encourage and disciple them?'

The members of the Board were eventually satisfied.

'This is something we should definitely be involved in,' said one.

'Yes, it's exactly what we need,' agreed another.

And so the motion was passed and Big Brothers and Sisters of Cambodia officially became a part of the Evangelical Fellowship of Cambodia's Youth Commission. Brian clapped me on the back as I left and with a lopsided grin said, 'You got it.'

There was now no looking back. Brian and Seila and I began to meet regularly and I endeavoured to explain the vision for a social movement to them. It would have to be something led by the Holy Spirit, responding to the opportunities given by God, resourced by the local church rather than from outside. I didn't want to be locked into a bureaucratic, logical framework, blueprint approach that would suck the life and spirit out of the movement.

We planned that we would share the vision for Big Brothers and Sisters at youth camps and youth conferences throughout the year. Afterwards, youth who felt God was calling them to get involved should return to their home church and speak to their pastor about it. If the pastor, youth leaders and youth themselves were keen, they would extend an invitation from their church to us to come and train the youth group. This training would take two or three days and at the end of the training, together with the pastor and youth leaders we would interview and screen those who wished to become Big Brothers or Big Sisters. The next step would be to liaise with the local village chiefs and the pastor to choose needy orphans from the surrounding community. We specified that these orphans should be unrelated to the Big Brothers and Sisters (I was picturing people choosing their nephew or cousin or something) and they should also be unchurched, since presumably the church would already be helping the orphans in their own congregation.

Once matched up, the Big Brothers and Sisters would meet together at least once a month for prayer and visit their little brothers and sisters at least once a week.

After a couple of false starts, we ended up with two young coordinators of the movement. Both had served as volunteer Big Brothers and Sisters and they became permanent fixtures around the Youth Commission office.

One day we organized a big picnic for all the Big Brothers and Big Sisters as well as their orphaned little brothers and sisters at a waterfall a couple of hours south of Phnom Penh. As they lounged on the grass, for many a first, some of the youth led a few songs of worship. Afterwards, I got up to bring a message of God's love to the kids as I often did on these occasions. I shared about a little orphan girl named Esther who God raised up to become the Queen of Persia and used to save the people of Israel from execution. Then I made it personal, 'God can use you too. No matter what anyone says about you, no matter what people call you. God loves orphans and he has an awesome plan for your life. He is looking, searching for children who are willing to follow him. I believe that God wants to raise some of you up to become great leaders in this country. Some of you will become Christian business people, some of you will become Christian teachers, some of you will become pastors and evangelists!' I was getting carried away with the moment. 'In fact, sitting right here today could be the first Christian Prime Minister of Cambodia!' All the children and their Big Brothers and Sisters laughed wholeheartedly at the idea that one of them could become the Prime Minister. Some shook their heads.

But right at the back, a tough little girl named Molica raised her hand high up in the air and declared with all the confidence she could muster, 'That's me, Uncle Craig! That's me!'

I was almost overcome with emotion as I looked at her pixie-like face. At thirteen years of age I knew Molica had already nursed her mother to her death by AIDS and now her father was getting sicker. Molica was responsible for going to the market each morning and buying the food which she would later cook for her father and two younger brothers. With help from Project HALO, Molica was able to stay in school, but only just. It would be a miracle if she were to finish high school, let alone university and one day become the Prime Minister of Cambodia. But in my heart I knew that if the God of the Bible could take a little orphan girl named Esther, and raise her up to become Queen of a foreign land as part of God's wonderful plan to save the nation of Israel, then that same God could also take a little orphan girl named Molica and raise her up to become the first godly Prime Minister of a broken and torn nation such as Cambodia, to bring healing and hope to her people.

Molica's Big Sister smiled at her and though I couldn't hear from the front, I imagined she mouthed the words, 'Yes. I believe you could too.'

Gutted by Betrayal

As Project HALO and the Big Brothers and Sisters of Cambodia ministry began to take off, the spiritual warfare increased. With Kristin and Susan leaving for a year's sabbatical, I was asked to take on the role of Servants Cambodia Team Leader. The role involved investing more time in the expatriate and Cambodian teams. It also meant overseeing a wide variety of Servants projects, not just Project HALO.

The Servants team had established a variety of ministries over the course of more than a decade living amongst the urban poor in Cambodia and were now reaching thousands of people every year through these projects.

These included a vibrant ministry called The Little Conquerors, or TLC, that worked with more than a hundred disabled children and their families in the slums of our district. The Nutrition Project focused on malnourished children. The Community Sanitation Project worked with local schools and urban poor communities to build toilets and wells. Our Women's Health Project ran the brothel clinic as well as working with traditional birth attendants in caring for pregnant women and other aspects of women's health. And of course, we were involved in the whole spectrum of AIDS ministry, right from education through to homecare for people with HIV and AIDS, and then the orphan care in Project HALO.

One of our major goals during this period was to finally officially hand over the various Servants projects to our Cambodian co-workers, the full-time Christian staff such as Aunty Lin, who were already running things day to day, and overseeing the hundreds of volunteers from various projects. This had been a lengthy process, including many years of discipleship and mentoring, coaching and training. They were keen to establish themselves as a local Cambodian NGO, with their own name and constitution.

Our Cambodian counterparts had been through a protracted and harrowing process of negotiation with the government in order to register as a local Cambodian organization. We held a huge celebration to which we invited 400 people, everyone from orphans and disabled people to local pastors and government officials. Every staff member and volunteer was decked out in the new maroon T-shirt, with TASK, the name they had decided to call themselves (a Cambodian acronym meaning Health and Development for the Poor), emblazoned across the back. It was a day of great pride and glory to God. One local government representative got up and made a speech saying how grateful he was to the Christians for doing this kind of work.

The TASK folks had elected two co-directors and a deputy to lead the organization. These godly men would lead for three years and then another election would be held for new leadership. As expatriates we would continue to support and mentor our Cambodian counterparts but the control would be in their hands. It was sink or swim time.

One day, just a few months after the official handover, Pauv, one of the co-directors, shared with me some concerns he had about a particular purchase of ten bicycles and some incorrect receipts made by Aunty Lin. 'The auditor picked up some discrepancies and I have asked Aunty Lin to account for these bicycles,' he said.

'Pauv, don't be too hard on her,' I chided. 'I'm sure it's all above board.'

But Pauv kept digging and found several more suspicious receipts. Eventually Pauv and two other staff went to the bicycle shop to ask about them. The bicycle shop owners denied all knowledge of the receipts and showed how they had clearly been altered. There was a sick feeling growing in my stomach.

We had to confront Aunty Lin and they called a meeting for the following morning. We sat in stony silence around on the floor in the office. No one knew what to say. Then someone started describing the steps leading up to uncovering the falsified receipts. I willed him to get on with it. Finally, they looked to me, expectant.

In one of the blackest moments of my life, I turned to Aunty Lin and with a trembling voice said, 'Did you falsify these receipts?' Silently I implored her to give a good reason for the discrepancy, something I could latch onto, anything to not make what now seemed inevitable come to pass.

'Yes. I did,' she mumbled softly. The woman I had invested the last few years of my life in training and mentoring was looking at the ground, guiltily.

'Why?' I pleaded, tears welling. 'Why would you do this? How could you do this?' I was on the verge of breaking down in emotion. I felt betrayed, but more than that I felt desperately sad for Aunty Lin. 'You must know TASK has a zero tolerance policy on this kind of thing?'

'I know. I know the rules. I know I'll have to go,' she whispered. And that was that. We had officially handed over leadership of Project HALO to TASK along with all the other projects several months before. It was no longer in my hands and the decision to fire Aunty Lin was made according to the rules that had been mutually agreed by everyone, including Aunty Lin. She had helped make the very rope that hanged her. Together we agreed not to go to the police, but the money she had taken was repaid out of her pension fund.

The hundreds of families in Project HALO were outraged. There was even briefly talk of protests and petitions. After all, Aunty Lin had become a huge part of their lives and this kind of thing was normal and expected in Cambodia. Emotionally, I was gutted. In private, I wept bitterly and I raged, knowing I was partly to blame. After all, I had set up the cash-handling systems for what had become a huge project. I was responsible for placing before her the temptation she had ultimately given in to. Who was to say I might not have done the same thing on a meagre salary handling a big budget? How could restoration, grace and forgiveness be found?

Within days Pauv was showing me the new financial system they had been working on to avoid this kind of thing ever happening again. We asked a British accountant with expertise in this area to look it over and he made suggestions as well. But though the new tighter systems were in place, ensuring strict accountability, it was all too late to save Aunty Lin from falling.

Aunty Lin's departure left a huge gap – in the ministry, in my heart and in the lives of hundreds of children. I offered to step back in temporarily as Project Manager, but Pauv and the other leaders of TASK felt that having an expatriate take over again would be a step backwards. I was proud of these godly men and women and they gave me confidence that in future crises, which would surely come, they would be able to handle things just fine.

We were still in need of a new leader though. One of the biggest problems we faced was trying to work out where all the families lived. We had almost a thousand children in the project at that time and because they were divided between Aunty Lin and Big Brother La for oversight, we had to track down over half. Luckily, since they had all been referred from the AIDS homecare program, we could ask the homecare volunteers to show us most. (There are no addresses in the slums.) Some had moved, and it took us several weeks to get the database back in shape again. During this time, a talented young Cambodian woman from another Servants project took over and we worked together to lay stronger foundations. We decided that the Project HALO team needed a couple more people to help ease the huge workload.

Eventually the decision was made to appoint Big Brother La as the leader of Project HALO. He was a great worker with a good heart, and with some restructuring and a couple more people to ease the massive workload, I was confident that Project HALO would continue to grow and impact the lives of hundreds of urban poor and their orphans. With a sense of relief I realized that by God's grace we had survived a major crisis relatively unscathed and come out the other side even stronger and wiser than before.

Kicked Out, Again

During the Aunty Lin crisis, Nay gave birth to our second child, a beautiful baby girl we named Micah. With that new life we both began to sense that God was calling us into a new phase of ministry. More change was in the pipeline. Around that time I was asked to become the International Coordinator of Servants, leading the movement my mentor Viv Grigg had founded and recruited me into. We were being faced with the fact that we would need to leave Cambodia in order to do more travel. Nay and I spent long periods wrestling with God in prayer and eventually came to see God's promise in the midst of the upheaval: if we would be willing to step back from the coalface, he would use us to raise up hundreds more workers more to take our places in the Asian harvest.

It was a heart-wrenching decision to leave the place God had called me to more than ten years prior, the nation he had called Nay to return to since childhood. It was the country we had called home with our two children for over six years.

One day, with just months to go before we departed Phnom Penh to relocate to Canada, the village chief's wife came to see us. Our slum at the End of the Road was being evicted, she said. The huge old apartment buildings we lived in had finally been deemed unsafe for human habitation and were being slated for demolition.

Nay and I laughed afterwards to think that they were trying to evict us for the second time in Cambodia. Too late, we were leaving! We got involved in helping our neighbours link with the UN to negotiate for compensation from the government, who had already sold the land out from under us to a real estate developer.

The orphans of Project HALO were in good hands. Over four hundred children affected by AIDS had graduated from Project HALO or moved away, no longer needing our help. Another 600 were currently being served. The first orphans were beginning to go to university and get married. Some had even had kids! Hundreds of children, their families and their neighbours had been touched by the gospel of the kingdom, and we had seen lives truly transformed by Christ.

The new Project HALO team, under the guidance and support of the rest of the TASK and Servants folk, would be in God's care. To our delight, Big Brother La was engaged to be married to Guntee from Young Life and they asked us to do their pre-marital counselling. A bunch of new team members from Australia, New Zealand and the Philippines would be arriving the following year to join the Servants team and they would add their own creativity and expertise to the mix.

Vibrant communities of believers had been catalyzed in Vee's village and other places and the Big Brothers and Sisters of Cambodia movement had been sparked and was beginning to spread like wildfire through church youth groups all over the land. We praised God for what he had done, despite our weaknesses and doubts.

The story all began very simply really. Just by moving into the neighbourhood. But then, that's how Jesus kicked things off too, when the Word became flesh and pitched his tent among us.

Now we sensed Jesus was leading us to a move into a new neighbourhood, to establish a Servants team in the inner city of Vancouver. We wanted to find out how these biblical principles he had given us, incarnation, simplicity, holism, servanthood and community, would apply in the West, on the downtown Eastside.

Postscript: A Call to Action

The Would-be Witch Doctor is long dead and I am going to see his widow, years after we first moved into this Cambodian slum and became neighbours and then friends.

The lane is lined with ramshackle huts made from salvaged corrugated iron and second-hand wood, including the house that we once called home. A group of men sit playing cards in the shadows and women sell small packets of food from the front of their tiny houses. At the end of this path to the north lies Victory Creek, now a three metre wide open sewer canal crawling with vermin and rancid with disease. The heat is brutal, the air is thick, and there is no shade, not a tree in sight.

At first no one notices the arrival of a tall foreigner with shaggy brown hair and his shorter Chinese-looking wife. But then a child somewhere shouts, 'Uncle Craig! Aunty Nay!' and the children gather round, grabbing our arms joyfully. Others, who in our absence have grown into gangly teens, look on with self-conscious grins. Grey-haired women smile the same toothless smiles and nod their heads in greeting. Nay is soon busy chatting with an old neighbour and I leave her to go and visit the Would-be Witch Doctor's widow.

Nudging open the wooden door of her house, my eyes struggle to adjust to the darkness inside after the brilliant sunshine. I suppose she will be hard at work preparing lunch for her Down's syndrome son, Bo. In the corner of the room I imagine an altar will be standing in remembrance of her dead husband, who tried hard to be a *kru kmae* or traditional healer, but was never recognized by the community. Perhaps some day-old bananas or some wilting flowers will be placed there as an offering to appease his ghost. In my nostrils I can almost smell the sickly sweet aroma of incense sticks burning to placate the territorial spirits.

Slowly, my eyes find focus and looking around the room I catch my breath, unsure whether to believe what I am seeing.

- A group of perhaps ten or fifteen men and women are sitting in a circle on the floor.
- Each one has an open Bible in their lap and they are worshipping Jesus in song.

Incredulous, I look at the widow, seated on the far side of the circle. I can see immediately that she is no longer the same person. Her face, especially her tired eyes, has been transformed by joy and she looks up at me with a smile that simply declares, 'God is good.' A fledgling church has been birthed in this, the Would-be Witch Doctor's house, what was once the very centre of despair in the slum.

I pen the words of this book in the closing days of our time in Cambodia. On my mind are the children of the urban poor in cities all over Asia who live in spiritual and physical darkness. Children who have seen the benefits of Asia's economic boom, but only from the curb side as they watch the Land Cruisers speed by. Children who do not yet know the love of their Father in heaven. Children who will scavenge scraps and beg a pittance from passers-by in order to put food in the rice bowl that evening. By tomorrow morning, 30,000 of those children will have died.

I believe God's heart is breaking over each and every one of those children, each and every family who came to the city full of hopes and dreams, and instead found only misery and injustice. And his call is this: 'If anyone would come after me, he must deny himself and take up his cross and follow me.'

Jesus said 'the poor you will always have with you,' and I believe that this is because as followers of Jesus we are called to follow him into those places of poverty. To be friends with the poor, to go where Jesus would go and do what Jesus would do. Some he will call to follow him to the poorest countries of the world. But our richest nations also have dark corners to which Jesus would go: inner-city poverty and sadness, addiction, homelessness, prostitution and brokenness.

The church has been slow to respond to the call to practice true compassion, to suffer alongside, to follow Jesus into the dark places. Preferring instead to keep the poor at arm's length, we have chosen service delivery and charity over real relationships. This allows us to maintain our lifestyles, while feeling good about our generosity.

But now, like embers glowing red in the darkness, all over the world I am sensing an awakening. A new generation of young people who aren't interested in chasing a life of middle class mediocrity, 2.4 kids and a picket fence. The old categories of evangelism versus social action are meaningless to this generation; word and deed are inseparable. It is a generation committed to integrity. This new generation are willing to sacrifice everything in order to serve Jesus. They are willing to be more than just admirers of Jesus. They are willing to be followers.

These followers will seek out like-minded others and build community together. They will aspire to live simple and gentle lives of beauty and grace in hard places. They will go as teams into some of the darkest corners of the earth: the slums of Asia's megacities, the inner cities and ghettoes of the so-called developed world.

And the old-school missions dichotomy of 'home' and 'field' will be meaningless because the field is right where they live. Wherever there is suffering and hurt, poverty and injustice they will be there, like Jesus. They will see God's grace and his divine spark in the faces of the children, the homeless, the drug addicted and the alcoholic. Ironically, it is in those places of suffering, poverty and death that they will discover Jesus.

Appendix 1: Servants to Asia's Urban Poor

Servants to Asia's Urban Poor is an international movement of radical followers of Jesus, a network of teams living and ministering in the slums of the megacities of Asia for almost twenty-five years. It was started by Viv Grigg, who was working as a missionary in Manila and who, over a period of four years, became increasingly burdened by the desperate situation of the millions of poor in the city. He was astounded to find no protestant missionary living in the slums. And so, he became the first, renting a room in the squatter settlement of Tatalon. Out of that came a movement to reach the poorest of the poor in cities all over Asia and now the world: Servants to Asia's Urban Poor. Our vision is to see the urban poor and their communities transformed by Christ.

Servants workers are motivated by a common set of five biblical principles:

1. **Incarnation:** we live with the urban poor, learning from them, building genuine relationships, participating in their lives and struggles, learning their language and their culture, and working out how Jesus' love can best be shown in their context.
2. **Community**: as well as a commitment to the communities we move into, we have a passion to work

together in supportive teams that model the love, care and community that Jesus spoke of. We work with people, not just for them.

3. **Wholism**: we have a God who is working 'to redeem all things' and to restore wholeness of life to rich and poor alike. We work for justice, proclaim God's grace, and lift all things to him in prayer. We want to see the good news of Jesus proclaimed in word, deed and power.

4. **Servanthood**: we seek to follow him who came in humility 'not to be served but to serve', the only path to true leadership. We seek to empower the poor by placing control in their hands and not overpowering them with outside resources or expertise. We are pre-pared to embrace sacrifice and suffering, the only way to faithfully share in the life of Jesus and the poor.

5. **Simplicity**: we commit ourselves to lifestyles of inner and outward simplicity, setting aside our 'right' to affluence while there are still those who live in abject poverty. We desire to be a relevant yet prophetic voice in a world preoccupied with self.

These five Ministry principles are held in creative ten-sion with our five Community Values:

1. **Grace**: All that we do and are is rooted and sustained by God's lavish, unearned love, favour and forgive-ness towards us. This profound grace delivers us from unhealthy striving, competition and condemnation of ourselves or judgement of others.

2. **Celebration**: Directing our celebrations to God in worship, we look for excuses to throw parties, consciously marking every milestone and achieve-ment – no matter how small! We want to be people of generosity, who refuse to take ourselves too seriously.

3. **Beauty**: In our lives, in our homes, in our communities and in our world, we honour God and renew our souls by recognizing and creating beauty. In particular, we want to see and celebrate the beauty inherent in ourselves and in each other.

4. **Creativity**: By allowing our senses, our imaginations, our minds and bodies to fulfil their God-given potentials for creativity, we glorify God. We believe it does our souls good (and pleases God) when we create, through writing and storytelling, poetry, cooking, music, painting and other art forms.

5. **Rest**: God calls us to regular rhythms of work, rest and reflection – weekly Sabbaths and regular holy-days (holidays). We seek to obey God's command to rest in order to be refreshed, to be still and to deepen our relationship with him and one another.

For more information about Servants to Asia's Urban Poor see our website (www.servantsasia.org) or for a bit of human contact email us on info@servantsasia.org.

Appendix 2: Notes on Orphan Ministry

After several years of rapid growth and expansion in the ministry of Project HALO I felt it was important to take the time to evaluate and reflect on orphan care in Cambodia and document some of the lessons learned. A postgraduate degree in Community Development gave me just the excuse I needed to carry out a major research project looking at orphans in different types of care.

The research I conducted included visiting almost every orphanage in Phnom Penh, as well as doing in-depth interviews with 300 orphans: 150 orphans living in orphanages and 150 orphans living in the community. I also interviewed a number of the founders and directors of orphan projects in Cambodia in order to better understand the processes they went through in establishing their ministries.

In this section, I want to summarize those findings as well as draw on learning from Project HALO and the wider literature in order to assist those who sense a calling to work amongst orphans. This section may also be of benefit to churches and individuals who are supporting orphan ministry in some way and wish to be more informed.

I have already touched briefly on some of the research which establishes a strong argument that orphanage care can result in a number of negative impacts on orphans, including significantly increased levels of social maladjustment, aggression, attention demanding behaviour, sleep disturbance, extremes of over-affection or repelling affection, social immaturity and tendency to depression. My own observations have backed up these findings.

For example, Bender, who was eventually able to observe and study more than five thousand deprived children, once conducted a study of 250 children from extremely poor backgrounds. Many of these children had been in orphanages from infancy. Dr Bender and her research associate found that when many of these orphanage children were later placed in foster families they had difficulty accepting love or playing with other children. They also noticed that these children tried hard to get contact with adults but were not gratified by these interactions. The researchers followed up ten of these children later in life and found that all ten still had problems adjusting and relating to others.[71]

Dr Bender went on to conduct a number of studies testing the theory that growing up in an orphanage has an adverse effect on personality development. For example, she looked at 15 adolescents who had lived all their lives in an orphanage. She matched these children up by age, sex and parental background with 15 children who had grown up in foster homes. She claimed that the differences between the two groups were stunning. The institutionalized children were markedly lower in intelligence, social maturity, concentration and school achievement than the similar children in foster homes.

Lowrey conducted another study of 28 children who had lived in orphanages for significant periods of their childhood and found that all the children displayed symptoms of inadequate personality development such as aggression, attention-demanding behaviour, sleep disturbance, over-affection and repelling affection. In particular, Lowrey noticed a low level of speech development in all the children.[72] Goldfarb did a similar comparison of 40 orphanage children with 40 similar orphans who had grown up in foster homes. Goldfarb used a checklist of behavioural problems and found that the orphanage children all exhibited a variety of these symptoms while only a third of the other children who had been in foster homes exhibited symptoms. The most common behavioural problem he observed was hyperactivity.

The research shows that the younger the child, the worse the effects of orphanage care. For example, Gindl, Hetzer and Sturm used a developmental age test to examine 20 infants under the age of two who had been in an orphanage for at least six months. They found that the mean developmental quotient for these children was significantly lower (ten points lower) than for a similar group of children who were brought up in inadequate homes.[73]

A more recent study compared 25 randomly selected young children from an orphanage in Romania to 11 similar children in the community. Kaler and Freeman used a range of developmental tests to test the children. Results showed that the children in the orphanage all displayed significantly lower levels of cognitive and social development. They found no connection between low scores and birth weight, age at entry to the orphanage or length of time in the institution. In contrast, the community-based children were functioning at normal level for social interaction, communication and play.[74]

A study conducted in Lebanon backed up these observations about the impact of orphanage care on younger children. Dennis followed up formerly institutionalized children in Lebanon. He was able to compare the IQ scores of children discharged and found a correlation between the age at adoption and IQ. According to his findings, the greater the age at adoption, the lower the eventual IQ. He concluded that institutionalized children should get out of the orphanage as quickly as possible![75]

Even older children are affected somewhat. A study conducted by Bodman and his colleagues compared 51 institutionalized teenagers with 52 similar school children of the same age. The school children had also lost parents and some had been displaced by war, but were living with their families. The researchers found that the institutionalized teenagers had less contact with the community, less contact with relatives and were eventually less successful in their careers.[76]

Other similar studies looked specifically at orphanages where there were adequate numbers of staff per child. For example, a Swedish researcher named Klackenburg studied a number of high quality orphanages where there was on average a nurse for every three children. However, Klackenburg found a statistically significant difference in emotional stability between the children in the orphanages and similar children in foster care.[77]

Likewise, Fischer studied 189 institutionalized children in a Catholic home where the children were given plenty of individual attention and adult interaction. Nevertheless, she found that a third of the children suffered emotional problems, particularly in the two extremes of passivity and hyperactivity.[78]

An interesting longitudinal study was carried out up until very recently tracking children at ages seven, eleven, sixteen, twenty-three and thirty-three. The researchers used a test called the 'Malaise Inventory' to measure tendency towards depression at the ages of twenty-three and thirty-three. Results showed that those who had spent time in orphanages had a greater tendency to depression than those who had not. Worried that other variables might be skewing their data, the researchers, Cheung and Buchanan, then attempted to remove other factors that might have impacted on this result, such as early experience of poverty. However, they still found that having been in an orphanage significantly impacted on the tendency to depression.

I have also briefly introduced Bowlby's 'attachment theory' which offers a partial reason for these sad results, suggesting that many of these difficulties result from the lack of availability of appropriate, nurturing, stable 'mother substitutes' in orphanages and orphan homes.

Orphanage care also lacks sustainability due to its relatively high costs compared to community-based care and is seriously limited by building size and staff numbers. Orphanages and children's homes take away the responsibility for orphan care from the wider community thereby reducing the amount of community participation and ownership and sending a message that poor communities are not capable of caring for orphans. Children are separated from their families and communities and raised in situations which do not prepare them for life as an adult. Finally, children are more likely to lose any inheritance of land or property if they are not present to protect these assets from unscrupulous neighbours or relatives.

The alternative, community-based care, still carries some risk of abuse and stigmatization, and those who provide the care often lack support and resources. However, these shortcomings can be partially met and mitigated by well-informed organizations. Community-based care offers orphaned children the opportunity to maintain a sense of connectedness to their extended family and community, a vital source of solace and support. The approach allows greater levels of community and child participation and is inherently more sustainable. Finally, as Christians, community-based care allows us to impact the entire community for Christ, not just a select group of children being raised in a cloistered environment.

Children already living in orphanages and children's homes must not be ignored or forgotten. Neither do these institutions need to be abandoned. But a radical reorientation will be required to transform them into community-focused centres for orphan and family support. This de-institutionalization process cannot happen overnight, but should proceed in stages.

De-Institutionalization Phase 1: Gatekeeping

First, the grounds for placement in the orphanage are re-examined. It is a well-established fact that in reality, the majority of children are being admitted for reasons of poverty. 'Gatekeeping', the process of assessment which should precede admission into residential care, needs to be strengthened and consistently applied. According to Article 9 of the UN Convention on the Rights of the Child, children with living parents and extended family should not be accepted into residential care except in cases of abuse. In the light of that, the following is a useful list of questions that should be asked before admission[79]

- Why does the child need alternative care?
- What is the opinion of the child?
- How does the child feel?

- Does the child have particular experiences (abuse, war experiences, etc.) that need special follow-up, and how will they be dealt with?
- Is the institution competent in helping the child?
- Does the child have siblings who are already in the institution or have been admitted at the same time?
- What has the child been told about the admission and its causes? Does the child believe what she/he has been told?
- How was the child prepared for admission?
- What other alternatives have been tried or considered?
- What is the benefit of the institution for the child? How does it benefit the family?
- What will the care plan be and how long will the child need to stay?
- How will the situation of the child and his/her family be reviewed?
- Why can't the child stay at home?
- What support would be needed for the child to live at home? Who can provide this?
- What is the plan for family and community contact? What are the child's expectations regarding this?
- Are there any signed documents regarding the placement of the child?
- Does the child have a guardian external to the institution?

Where parents are merely poor and quite admirably, but mistakenly, seeking a better life for their children in residential care, every effort should be made to work closely with these parents in order to help them raise their standard of living and reach a level where they are able to provide for their children's needs. Parents need to know that financial provision is not as important as the emotional loving relationship they can offer the child, which cannot be so readily given in an institution. Nevertheless, helping parents to understand this can go hand in hand with a sound developmental strategy to help families improve their living standards.

Where children have lost both parents, there are almost always relatives who would be available to care for the orphans with encouragement and sometimes some low level of material support. Every effort should be made to provide support to those extended family members who are deemed suitable caregivers for their orphaned relatives.

De-Institutionalization Phase 2: Reunification

The next stage involves family tracing and reunification of those children who are able to return to their families and communities. For some children living in orphanages, straightforward reunification with family or relatives will be possible, especially where poverty was the key component of their original placement. However, income generation activities or some form of sustainable material support will almost certainly be needed in order to rectify the original situation which led them to the placement. Donors who have been supporting orphanages should consider redirecting their support to these families in order to encourage the institution to move towards a greater community focus.

Before reunification takes place, each case should be carefully examined by a social worker in conjunction with the orphanage staff to ensure that the reunification is appropriate. The children themselves should be listened to and their opinions should be taken into account.

De-Institutionalization Phase 3: Long Term Foster Care

Many children admitted to institutional care have a chronic illness such as HIV/AIDS, have experienced traumatic losses and/or serious abuse, and may also have physical or learning disabilities. These are children who need special help and attention regarding their development and well-being. However, very often the capacity and structure of institutions means that they are not able to meet the needs of these children or fulfil their rights to rehabilitation. In cases of abuse, serious disease, disability or other situations where the biological family is unsuited or unable to care for a child, every effort should be made to find a suitable adoptive or long-term foster family in a community context. This will ensure that the child has an ongoing 'mother substitute' and the appropriate nurture and care. The only case where a child should be admitted to institutional care is where they require highly specialized care that cannot be provided in any other setting and this should be as temporary as possible, much like a hospital stay. Some development theorists have suggested that such may be the case with some children infected with the HIV/AIDS virus who are receiving antiretroviral treatment. However, the need for nurturing adult relationships such as described by Bowlby's attachment theory is still an unresolved issue even in these rare cases if deemed justifiable.

De-Institutionalization Phase 4: Community-Focus

What was originally the orphanage now functions as a community-focused centre for the support of struggling families and their children. Much of this work will be following up the children that were previously in the institution. However, increasingly, the client base will expand as other vulnerable families are identified and development initiatives are undertaken. The orphanage staff are retrained as social workers or released to pursue other work.

Endnotes

1 Bonk, J. *Missions and Money: Affluence as a Western Missionary Problem* (New York: Intercultural Publications Inc, 1991), 45.

2 United Nations Human Settlements Program, *The Challenge of Slums: Global Report on Human Settlements* 2003 (London: Earthscan Publications, 2003).

3 Grigg, V., *Companion to the Poor: Christ in the Urban Slums* (Waynesboro: Authentic and World Vision, 2004).

4 The term 'compassion' comes from the Latin words *cum* and *pati*, which mean 'to suffer with'. According to Henri Nouwen compassion means going directly to those people and places where suffering is most acute and building a home there.

5 John 20:21.

6 Mark 8:34. These thoughts on the incarnation and the cross are well articulated by Jonathan Bonk in *Missions and Money* (1991).

7 The words of Ita Ford, Catholic missionary murdered in El Salvador, 1980.

8 A prophetic act of 'redemptive suffering', which would be undertaken out of responsible concern to overcome others' greater suffering might be even more worthwhile than the pragmatic benefits which were more immediately obvious.

9 UNICEF/USAID/UNAIDS, *Children on the Brink 2004: A Joint Report on Orphan Estimates and Program Strategies* (Washington, DC: UNICEF/USAID/UNAIDS, 2004a),12.

[10] UNICEF/USAID/UNAIDS, *Children on the Brink* (2004a), 25.

[11] About 27 per cent of children born to HIV positive mothers are infected by the virus. The most dangerous time for transmission is during the birthing process, though transmission can also occur through breast milk.

[12] These thoughts are clearly articulated in Keenan, J., *Moral Wisdom: Lessons and Texts from the Catholic Tradition* (New York: Rowman & Littlefield Publishers Inc., 2004).

[13] Khmer HIV/AIDS NGO Alliance KHANA, *Appraisal of Needs and Resources for Children Affected by HIV/AIDS in Cambodia* (UK: NAM Publications, 2001).

[14] Alkenbrack, S., *The Social and Economic Impact of HIV/AIDS on Families and Children in Cambodia* (POLICY Project. PowerPoint presentation at Sunway Hotel, Phnom Penh, Cambodia, 23 August 2004).

[15] Alkenbrack, *Social and Economic Impact* (2004).

[16] Alkenbrack, *Social and Economic Impact* (2004).

[17] Alkenbrack, *Social and Economic Impact* (2004).

[18] Carswell, K., *The psychosocial wellbeing of orphans and vulnerable children in the Thai/Cambodia border areas* (PowerPoint presentation at Sunway Hotel, Phnom Penh, Cambodia, 23 August 2004).

[19] Carswell, *Psychosocial Wellbeing* (2004).

[20] Carswell, *Psychosocial Wellbeing* (2004).

[21] Save the Children, *A Last Resort: The growing concern about children in residential care* (London: International Save the Children Alliance, 2004), 1.

[22] Dybdal, A.S. and G. Daigle, *The national survey of providers of alternative care for children in Cambodia: Survey Report* (Phnom Penh: MOSALVY/UNICEF, 2002), 15

[23] KHANA, *Appraisal of Needs and Resources* (2001)

[24] A similar discrepancy was found between the views of adults and children in Malawi. Mann, G., *Family Matters: The Care and Protection of Children Affected by HIV/AIDS in*

Malawi (New York: International Save the Children Alliance, 2002), cited in Williamson, J., *A family is for a lifetime* (Washington, DC: The Synergy Project, USAID, 2004) Article 12 of the UN Convention on the Rights of the Child states that children have a right to participate in decisions that affect them in accordance with their maturity and understanding (1989, available online at:
http://www.unicef.org/crc/accessed January 2006). This right to participate in decisions should be applied according to the age, experience and understanding of the child concerned.

[25] Dybdal and Daigle, *National survey* (2002), 6.

[26] UNICEF/USAID/UNAIDS, *Children on the Brink* (2004a), 25.

[27] Dybdal and Daigle, *National survey* (2002), 59.

[28] Dybdal and Daigle, *National survey* (2002), 16.

[29] Chinn, S., *The HOSEA Project survey of alternative care in Phnom Penh and Kandal Province, Cambodia 2002* (Phnom Penh, Cambodia: unpublished, acquired from the author September 2005), chart 3.1 and see also Dybdal and Daigle, National survey (2002), 16.

[30] Dybdal and Daigle, *National survey* (2002), 16

[31] KHANA, *Appraisal of Needs and Resources* (2001).

[32] Chinn, S. The HOSEA *Project survey of the level and quality of child-care in the temples of Kandal Province, Cambodia 2004* (Phnom Penh, Cambodia: unpublished, acquired from the author September 2005), 9.

[33] HOSEA,*Child – Care in the Temples* (2004), 9.

[34] A selection of representative studies have been included in Appendix 1.

[35] Provence, S., and Lipton, R., *Infants in institutions: a comparison of their development with family-reared infants during the first year of their life* (New York: International University Press, 1962).

[36] Yule, W., and N.V. Raynes, 'Behavioural Characteristics of Children in Residential Care in Relation to Indices of

Separation', *Journal of Child Psychology and Psychiatry and Allied Disciplines*, 13 (1972), 249-258.

[37] Zeanah, C.H., C.A. Nelson, N.A. Fox, A.T. Smyke, P. Marshall, S.W. Parker and S. Koga, 'Designing research to study the effects of institutionalization on brain and behavioral development: The Bucharest Early Intervention Project', *Development and Psychopathology*, 15 (2003), 885-907.

[38] Rutter, M., L. Andersen-Wood, C. Beckett, D. Bredenkamp, J. Castle and C. Groothues, 'Quasi-autistic patterns following severe early global privation', *Journal of Child Psychology and Psychiatry and Allied Disciplines*, 40 (1999), 537-549.

[39] Tolfree, D., *Roofs and Roots: The care of separated children in the developing world* (Aldershot, UK: Arena, 1995), 142.

[40] Later I found out that Mueller's foundation still cares for orphans and children at risk today, but they have abandoned the orphanage model as new research has come to light, indicating better approaches. They now endeavour to place children in foster homes.

[41] Bowlby, J., *Maternal care and mental health* (London: Her Majesty's Stationery Office, 1951).

[42] Bowlby, *Maternal Care* (1951),13.

[43] Freud, A. and D. Burlingham, *Infants without Families* (London: George Allen and Unwin Ltd., 1944).

[44] Dybdal and Daigle, *National survey* (2002), 50.

[45] HOSEA, *Alternative Care* (2002), 8.

[46] Dybdal and Daigle, *National survey* (2002), 51.

[47] Numerous studies support the observation that community-based solutions are a much more cost effective approach. The high costs involved in building and running residential facilities are cited by many as unsustainable: Desmond, C. and J. Gow, *The cost effectiveness of six models of care for orphan and vulnerable children in South Africa* (University of Natal, Durban: UNICEF: Health Economics and AIDS Research

Division, 2001); Desmond, C., and T. Quinlan, 'Costs of Care and Support' in K. Kelly, W. Parker and S. Gelb (eds.) *HIV/AIDS, Economics and Governance in South Africa: Key Issues in Understanding Response. A Literature Review* (Johannesburg: USAID/Cadre, 2002); Foster, G. (1999) 'Orphan care in Zimbabwe – a community response' *AIDS Analysis Africa*, 10, 2,14-15; Johnson, S., P. Modiba, D. Monnakgotla, D. Muirhead, and H. Schneider, *Home Based Care for People With HIV/AIDS in South Africa: What will it cost?* (Johannesburg: Centre for Health Policy, University of Witwatersrand, 2001); Loening-Voysey, H. and T. Wilson, *Approaches to caring for children orphaned by AIDS and other vulnerable children: Essential elements for a quality service* (Unpublished report for UNICEF by the Institute for Urban Primary Health Care, 2001); Wright, J., *Working on the Front Line: An Assessment of the Policy Context and Responses of AIDS Housing and Related Service Providers in the Durban Metropolitan Area* (Durban: Built Environment Support Group, 2001).

[48] HOSEA, *Alternative Care* (2002), 12.

[49] Save the Children, *A Last Resort* (2004), 9.

[50] UNICEF/USAID/UNAIDS, *The framework for the protection, care and support of orphans and vulnerable children living in a world with HIV/AIDS* (Washington, DC: UNICEF/USAID/UNAIDS, 2004b), 9.

[51] Save the Children, *A Last Resort* (2004), 9.

[52] HOSEA, *Alternative Care* (2002), 8.

[53] HelpAge International, *Forgotten Families: Older people as carers of orphans and vulnerable children* (Brighton: HelpAge International/International HIV/AIDS Alliance, 2003), 8.

[54] Family Health International, *Cambodia CAA (Children Affected by AIDS) Review Report* (Cambodia: USAID, 2002).

[55] Dybdal and Daigle, *National survey* (2002), 9.

[56] Treating fourteen cases of Sexually Transmitted Infection (STI), such as herpes, syphilis etc. has been shown to

prevent one case of AIDS, because STIs greatly increase the risk of HIV infection through open sores and broken skin.

[57] This list and these insights are well articulated by the MissionYear handbook, available from www.missionyear.org.

[58] Servants had a deal with the hospital to provide the drugs for free.

[59] UNICEF/USAID/UNAIDS, *Framework for the protection* (2004b), 9,16.

[60] The phrase 'wounded healers' is from Nouwen, H., *The Wounded Healer* (London: Darton, Longman and Todd Ltd., 1994)

[61] Dybdal and Daigle, *National survey* (2002), 96.

[62] Foster, G., 'Safety nets for children affected by HIV/AIDS in Southern Africa' in R. Pharoah (ed.) *A Generation at Risk? HIV/AIDS, Vulnerable Children and Security in Southern Africa* (South Africa: Monograph, 2004).

[63] World Health Organization, *The importance of caregiver-child interactions for the survival and healthy development of young children: a review* (China: Department of Child and Adolescent Health and Development, 2004), vii.

[64] Bowlby, *Maternal Care* (1951).

[65] Foster, 'Safety nets' (2004), 84.

[66] A number of successful community-based ministries have mobilized large numbers of community members to show practical compassion to orphans. For example, the FOCUS program in Zimbabwe has mobilized community volunteers to visit and encourage more than four thousand orphans.

[67] For example, the Bethany Project in Zimbabwe which works with 8,000 children.

[68] Foster, 'Safety nets' (2004), 66.

[69] Foster, 'Safety nets' (2004), 68.

[70] Another form of abuse is emotional. Children orphaned by AIDS may be particularly subjected to stigmatization. A

knee-jerk reaction would be to remove the children from the source of this stigma. However, it is doubtful whether removing a small number of children from communities is the answer to stigmatization in general. In fact, it may be argued that removing the object of stigmatization will increase discrimination overall because therefore there is a greater sense of mystery, and fear is reinforced by the perception that these people are isolated because they are highly contagious. It would be better to invest resources in educating communities about AIDS so that stigma is decreased. On the other hand, stigmatization can also occur solely because a child is in an orphanage or other institution. Studies have shown that children who are or have been in residential care are frequently stigmatized and discriminated against at school and by society. For example, the children who live in temples are often called 'temple dogs'.

[71] Bender, L. and H. Yarnell, 'An Observation Nursery', *American Journal of Psychiatry*, 97, (1941) 1158-74.

[72] Goldfarb, W., 'The Effects of Early Institutional Care on Adolescent Personality', *Journal of Experimental Education*, B, (1943), 106-129.

[73] Gindl, I., H. Hetzer, and M. Sturm, 'Unangemessenheit der Anstalt als Lebensraum fur das Kleinkind' *Angew Psycholog*, 52, (1937), 310-58.

[74] Kaler, S. and B.J. Freeman, 'Analysis of environmental deprivation: cognitive and social development in Romanian orphans' *Journal of Child Psychology and Psychiatry and Allied Disciplines*, 35, (1994) 4, 769-781.

[75] Dennis, W., *Children of the Creche: Conclusions and implications* (London: Open Books, 1976).

[76] Bodman, T.F., M. MacKinley and K. Sykes, 'The Social Adaptation of Institution Children', *The Lancet*, 1, (1950), 173-6.

[77] Klackenberg, G., 'Studies in maternal deprivation in infants' homes' *Paediatrics*, 45, (1956), 1-12..

[78] Fischer, L., 'Hospitalism in Six-Month-Old Infants' *American Journal of Orthopsychiatry*, 22, (1952), 522-33.

[79] Save the Children, *The Last Resort* (2004), 8.

Resources for Going Further

Learning more about working with orphans

David Tolfree's book, *Roofs and Roots: The care of separated children in the developing world*, remains one of the best texts on the subject of caring for orphans and other children at risk. Based on his extensive research, Tolfree emphasizes the importance of preventing separation, documents the typical shortcomings of residential care and discusses alternatives to it, de-institutionalization, and ways to improve residential care. Published by Arena (1995).

World Vision's HIV/AIDS Hope Initiative have an excellent training guide called *Mobilizing and Strengthening Community-led Care for Orphans and Vulnerable Children* for training up community volunteers to work with orphans. The guide includes 19 lesson plans covering topics from Memory Books and counseling to making wills, hygiene and education.

Viva Network's *CHRIS-CABA Journal* is a free online resource-exchange focusing on the special needs of Christians and Christian organisations working with children affected by HIV and AIDS. The Viva Network website has past issues of the journal and a wide range of other resources for working with children (www.viva.org).

Celebrating Children is a textbook and a training curriculum providing biblically-based material to equip people for effective work with children in difficult circumstances. It is a unique synthesis of secular and Christian insights and research in key areas of child development. Topics covered include: understanding the child in context; listening; risk and resilience; holistic mission; and program and staff development (www.celebratingchildrentraining.info).

Building Blocks is a set of tools, principles and strategies for working with orphans and vulnerable children. It includes a manual supporting community action, Building Blocks in Practice, and provides advice on health and nutrition, education, psychosocial support, and other topics. Available in a number of different languages for use in Africa and Asia, online from the International AIDS Alliance website (www.aidsalliance.org).

Tearfund UK has a comprehensive resource website for Christians working with children at risk, including a useful booklet called *Children in Residential Care and Alternatives*. Tearfund also publish *PILLARS* Guides which provide practical, discussion-based learning on community development in simple English. The Guides are designed for use in small community groups (www.tearfund.org/tilz).

Learning more about Incarnational Ministry with Servants to Asia's Urban Poor

Servants is looking for people of all ages, who are committed to living out the teachings of Jesus, to join new teams being established to live and work amongst the urban poor. If our vision, values and principles resonate with you, contact us and explore the possibility of serving long term with a Servants team.

Servants also accepts a limited number of people each year for short term internships in Asian (and some western) cities. Focussed on discovering more about God's heart for the poor, interns live in the slum with a local host family, meet regularly with the rest of the Servants team for prayer and support, and work through specially targeted readings and meditations under the guidance of an assigned mentor.

From time to time, Servants also conducts short training courses and workshops. Contact your local Servants team for more information (www.servantsasia.org).

Real Lives

D.J. Carswell

You are on a train; you look at the people around you. Someone hides behind a newspaper. Another dozes; a young man nods to the beat from his iPod. A baby cries further along the carriage and a table of football fans celebrate an away victory drinking a few cans of lager. Someone's mobile goes off; a student sitting next to you sends a text message. Eavesdropping on the conversations you catch soundbites from those around you. Who exactly are they, you wonder?

Real people
> **All different**
>> **Everyone with a life story**
> *Real lives*

In *Real Lives* you will meet, among others . . . a famous footballer . . . a sophisticated lady from South Africa . . . an Olympic athlete . . . a backpacker exploring the States . . . a Brahmin from India . . . a young, abused girl . . . the greatest man in history who was a child refugee . . . and the author's own story of a changed life.

ISBN: 978-1-85078-412-8

Available on www.authenticmedia.co.uk or from your local Christian bookshop

Stories from China
Fried Rice for the Soul

Luke Wesley

'I hope that everyone who desires to help the Chinese Church, whether living overseas or serving in China, might have a chance to read this book.'   *Brother Yun*

Stories from China is a collection of 52 inspirational stories that seek to illustrate the strength of the Chinese Church and convey the significant insights it offers to Christians in the West. A brief, introductory chapter gives a general overview of the Church in China and provides important context for the stories that follow. Each story is prefaced with a Scripture reading and concludes with a prayer. The book offers perspective on Chinese culture and Christianity, as well as devotional insights. *Stories from China* is geared for the general reader and will be meaningful to people from a wide range of denominational backgrounds.

Luke Wesley has lived and served in China for the past ten years. He is fluent in Mandarin Chinese and has ministered extensively in house church and TSPM church settings. He has helped establish a small network of house churches and currently serves as the director of an underground, residential Bible school in China that he founded.

ISBN: 978-1-85078-638-2

Available on www.authenticmedia.co.uk or from your local Christian bookshop

True Grit

Deborah Meroff

A wake-up call to crises facing women around the world, told through the exciting stories of nine courageous people and hard-hitting 'Vital Statistics' files.

This tells the inspiring true adventures of nine 'ordinary' women who are making a difference in such places as Tajikistan, India and Lebanon. We hear about Kathryn, a deaf American who built a ministry to the deaf in Israel; Pam, who lived and worked in war-racked Tajikstan, a country completely alien and unknown to Westerners; and Cindy who ended up returning as a missionary to Vietnam, a country from which she had had a dangerous escape as a teenager.

Fact files between stories highlight global female abuse, such as child brides, sex trafficking, girl soldiers and 'honour' killings. But the book does not stop there. *True Grit* goes on to point out simple ways for all of us to help turn the tide for women worldwide.

Deborah Meroff has travelled to over 80 countries in the last 18 years in her role of journalist-at-large for the mission organisation, Operation Mobilisation. She has written several books, plus dozens of articles in several countries and is a columnist for *Woman Alive* magazine.

ISBN: 978-1-85078-575-0

Available on www.authenticmedia.co.uk or from your local Christian bookshop

IMAGINE

Mark Greene

'Never before have we received such a wave of positive affirmation from a publication: "Wonderful." "Stunning, absolutely brilliant." "Truly inspired of the Lord" "Challenging, encouraging and immensely motivating"'

Joel Edwards, head of the Evangelical Alliance

How can we reach our nation? • And how can we create Christian communities that really support and equip their people? • Is there really a way forward?

Imagine is about daring to dream. The head of the London Institute for Contemporary Christianity, best-selling author Mark Greene presents a powerful vision for our culture. Visually pleasing, with a series of stunning photographs, he lays down a challenge to all Christians. In a country where people don't even know why Easter is a public holiday a radical strategy is desperately needed. *Imagine* is it.

'Should be required reading for every church leader in the UK, and great fuel for thought in small groups and away days.'

Andy Peck, Christianity + Renewal

'At last – a thorough look at what it means to be Christian. I hate being a Christian in church, while being unsure of what to be in work. Someone understands and is communicating to me in ways I understand. Wow! There is hope!'　　*Anonymous correspondent*

ISBN: 978-1-85078-544-6

Available on www.authenticmedia.co.uk or from your local Christian bookshop